【經典】
HUMANITY
【人文】

心光有愛
映照生命的幽谷

Turn On The Heart Lamp
Mapping The Deep Valley of Life

林幸惠──著　　張恭逢──英譯　　（中英雙語）

前言

在暗處看見光

當我們漫步走過世界，有人在小島度假中，突然被持槍威脅交出錢財，卻遇到有人出手相助，所以能無事平安回家。有人則是佯裝好意在機場，送你一包粉，就足夠讓你傾家蕩產遭受牢獄之災。

這世界充滿神奇又不可思議的事物，生命無時無刻都在接受挑戰，無常且短暫，所以人必須不斷地抉擇與判斷：哪些該做，哪些不該做，做了變得更好，或做了會變得更糟，或者現在做了很好，未來卻更糟。但遇到無可避免的，不能逃脫的情境，或面對不能改變的命運，也就是等於到了最後的機會，更要去實現最高的價值與最深的意義，但最重要的是對苦難採取什麼態度，用什麼態度來承擔苦痛；如何才能冷靜果斷地處理。

證嚴法師說：「逆境可遇不可求，不要浪費。」若還能對所有的遭遇，懷著淡定而超然的心，或由宗教信仰，或花草樹木，抑或是晨曦夕陽美美的一瞥，相信人都會得到一些安慰的。尼采說，「懂得為何而活的人，幾乎任何痛苦都可以忍受。」

即使在高牆內，相信只要覺察出困惑，給自己一個活下去的使命，發大心立大願，找出了利他奉獻的目標，堅持自己的意志力，就能增強忍受煎熬的耐力，也能轉動後悔又痛苦的情境，看見光芒。

有一天與友人去監獄送書，剛到大門口，朋友打電話來，問我在哪裡？我漫不經心地回她：「在監獄」，「嗄！妳怎麼了，發生什麼事啦？」朋友緊張又驚嚇地大叫，仿彿我已掉落地獄。

當我要回家時，突然又有朋友打來，「妳現在哪裡呀？」，「剛出監獄！」於是她屏息一下，接著小心翼翼地問：「那，妳沒事了噢？」

監獄，是一座在高牆內與世隔絕的地方，是犯下罪行的人，為他們的所作所為付出代價，而失去自由之處。因此談起監獄，總有一種恐怖又神祕的感覺。

可是，高牆外的人們還不曉得，牆內教誨師與各科員們，為了讓受刑人從錯誤中學習，在此轉捩站，以睿智和悲憫的眼光，用各種方法，諄諄教誨，幫助受刑人明辨是非，啟發人傷我痛的悲心，在未來出獄後能夠不再陷於誘惑，而免於兇惡，回歸社會步上有用的人生道路。教誨師們彷如是高牆內，指路的明燈，照亮著受刑人昏暗的心地。

這地球，沒有人是獨立存在的，所有人事物是連動的，每個選擇都會影響他人，即使是心靈的悸動，波瀾，微微的漣漪，都會產生所謂的蝴蝶效應，所以，每一個事件的發生，我們都多少有一點責任。但只要是能帶著善念，去做所有的決定，無形中也會促進人世間善的循環，因為蒼生安樂，自己才會得安樂。

感恩能執筆記錄監獄內教誨師與管理人們的慈悲，在採訪過程中，敘事故事的河流，出現著惆悵和憂傷，因為受刑人那些不為人知的祕密，都深藏在幽暗深處，由此造成了生命的風暴和潮汐。但教誨師們，時而菩薩低眉，滿懷悲憫，時而金剛怒目，策馬入林，但也無法置身事外，悲憫之心，發出的光芒，映照著教誨師們以真誠的愛在拔除苦難，在悠長的歲月中，苦口婆心地說盡了千言萬語，用盡了千方百計，只要有人幡然悔悟，就是對他們最大的餽贈了，因為只為眾生得離苦，是他們最大的使命。

此書中雖是真實案例，但均為化名，以保護個人隱私，希望藉此書的紀錄能啟發讀者，穿越紛雜的世相，看到這世界的苦難幽深的角落，明白了這世界，不是只圍繞著自己在轉。無論在何種情境下，無論身體是弱不禁風，或是健碩粗壯，只要不自羈絆，其實人還是有潛力，發揮自身的光芒，為社會盡一份心力，讓這個世界更美好。

在此讓我們一起來為《心光有愛》本書打開心的燈罩，拂去生活中的汙垢與灰塵，在本書的十八盞心燈中，一路指引著迷途人，但願最少有一盞燈，能點亮您與我，也能照亮周遭，令世間一切閃耀生輝。

讓我們一同來點亮這十八盞心燈

開燈了

請掀開燈罩，拂去心中的灰塵

推薦序

飛越高牆的青鳥

撰文 賴文玲（法務部矯正署宜蘭監獄教誨師）

「犯人不是關起來就好，幹麼去監獄關懷陪伴？」很多認識幸惠老師的人，一聽聞她近來老往監所跑，就不禁好奇地詢問。沒錯，監所是刑事司法執行的所在，也是普遍認為磁場不佳的陰晦角落，一想到那群刺龍刺鳳、罪無可赦的大哥，關他也只是剛好而已，怎會想要進來關心他們？

對於公平正義的伸張，人們能想到快速解決的方式，便是將罪犯審判、懲罰。然而，古代刑罰的「隔離主義」及「應報原則」雖符合一般人「以牙還牙、以眼還眼」的期許；但是，監禁囚犯真能消弭犯罪，讓這個社會變得更加美好？犯罪問題仍舊層出不窮，難道任其生生不息、永無止盡的輪迴？

美國國家科學院二〇一四年犯罪調查報告指出，長期監禁並無「預防效果」，監獄只是暫緩犯人再次犯罪的時間，無法有效阻止其出獄後再犯罪。犯罪成因錯綜複雜，犯罪現象只是反映社會整體的價值觀，如果一再用「次等公民」或「社會邊緣人」的排斥眼光，只會強化彼此的對立與仇視。所以，究竟要如何打擊犯罪？真的只能靜待警察抓壞人，白白浪費社會資源和成本？！

雖然犯罪學者主張：每個社會都有挫敗型的失序者，犯罪是社會的正常現象；但種種學說正說明：「貧窮」是社會難治的病，「低階層副文化」更是犯罪的溫床。實務研究也顯示：大部分受刑人處於社會底層，種種的悲劇造就他們有愛的缺口，甚至是早期創傷累積的受害者。等到長大後傷害自己或別人，來表達對社會不公的反擊，以獲得心理最初的補償。反思社會對低階層和弱勢者的冷漠鄙視，乃至對罪犯動輒處以刑責懲罰，似乎一勞永逸；然而，一代傳一代受挫經驗的複製，一件又一件矚目案件的發生，也逼著人們不得不省思，這個社會將付出多麼慘痛的代價！

監禁人犯於高牆和刺網內雖為必要之惡，但現代刑事政策趨向「矯正處遇」及「修復式正義」，認為隔離監禁是便宜之計，只會造成行為人對社會更加不滿和不平，引起更多對峙的紛爭和事端。以教育刑代替懲罰刑，並修復加害人、被害人與社區的關係，期許三面均贏，讓犯罪人順利復歸社會，才是司法處遇的最終目的。輔以「醫療預防模式」和「教化療癒理念」，把犯人當病人看待，當成個案好好輔導治療，讓他感受被陪伴、接納、包容，而願意做出改變的契機，才是杜絕再犯的根本之道。

慈濟志工團隊長期入監深耕，即是以人性關懷為立基點，落實「生命教育」和「品格教育」，以同理心去了解、傾聽和注視，期盼收容人在此脫胎換骨、改變宿命，回到社會上成為有用的人。慈濟人飛越刺絲高牆，樂當穿梭鐵窗的希望青鳥，相信唯有在感恩、尊重和愛中，拯救失落的靈魂才是生命的唯一出口。在這座被人遺忘的牢籠中，我望到人性最偉大的光輝，也看到人間最崇高的大愛！

在此也呼籲社會大眾，重新思考親子生活、教育體制、就業系統和社會福利等議題。司法是「社會道德的最後一道防線」，但公平正義必須建構於合適的家庭教育、學校教育、社會教育之上。社會應以慈濟為師，給予低階層和弱勢者關懷、支持與救助，絕對是刻不容緩之務，而逐次改善社會結構也是政府必須的作為。

　　欣聞幸惠老師的大作即將出版，這本老師辛勤走訪各監所，筆下描述的監所實況是如何樣貌？作學生的我引頸期盼。老師的無私奉獻深深感動著我，相信也會帶給讀者不同的見解和思考，若有進一步想為社會多做些什麼的悸動，那麼，老師辛勤筆耕的初衷，就已獲得滿滿的回報。在此感恩老師的愛心撰寫，也感恩大家的用心閱讀。

高牆內的十八盞心燈

撰文　江智超（實業家，慈濟志工）

因為參與慈濟志業，而認識幸惠師姊達二十年。身在醫生世家的幸惠師姐，家庭環境富裕，及長後從事醫藥業，事業有成，卻不喜奢華，常念蒼生，熱衷行善。三十年前毅然拋棄事業，立志追隨 證嚴上人，吸取 證嚴上人智慧精華，久經薰聞法香之後，便發願推廣靜思人文工作。近年來親證 上人智慧語錄，改變無數慈濟家庭，從唯我獨尊的貢高我慢，轉向感恩懺悔的慈濟大愛。讓師姊深深體悟到，醫病在醫心，醫心在開啟慧命，於是從醫業轉向筆耕，撰寫慈濟勵志書籍，借書傳法，與廣大會眾讀者，善結好緣。

近日有機會隨同師姊，在福建廣東地區，與慈濟志工菩薩分享心得。每一場分享，極富趣味溫馨，聽眾迴響激烈。尤其是 Q&A，問到人生難以圓滿的困境，除了用 上人的智慧回答之外，幸惠師姊會以其著作之書「用心祝福」才能「活出幸福」。希望疑惑者，借書中個案，來深切體會「用心的祝福」的意義，就是去我執，而達到智慧圓融的慈悲境界，指引大家找到幸福方向。

最近幸惠師姊，更是發揮了普天三無（天底下沒有我不愛的人，天底下沒有我不信任的人，天底下沒有我不原諒的人）精神，長期去監獄內，採訪對受刑人輔導的教誨師，他們如何為高牆內絕望的生命，澆灌出希望花朵。也藉著每一個案闡明出「心為工畫師」的佛法真義，一念為天堂，一念為地獄，天堂與地獄往往就在一念間。

為此，幸惠師姊集結教誨師們說的個案，以及管理者的心聲，著作成《心光有愛》一本書，當我細讀幾篇，文章內容，是借受刑人的故事，來警惕自我，人不要被情緒綑綁，不要被無名怒火燒心，才不會鑄下大錯。其次這本書，列舉了很多更生人教育工作者，開導一時犯下大錯之人，打開生命死結，找回自信，重新擁抱社會。相信人心本善，祇要有決心，善念開啟，便會自己掌控人生，活出奇蹟。

同時我們也要呼籲，以寬容心面對更生人，修補心靈創傷，更生人無法全靠自己力量就好起來，他們更需要社會以愛相陪。我們是不是要更有耐心，更有包容心的來引導他們走上一條光明之路。

同時，我們也要對於無辜的被害人及家屬感到憐惜，給予最大的照顧。幫助他們快速走出陰霾，療傷止痛。相信，社會上多一份愛，就少一份仇恨，讓這個社會更健康，更和諧。讓每個人都能感受大愛光照，如千年暗室，一燈能明。我也即興為這新著作寫了一則打油詩來祝福所有與這本書有緣的人：

　　高度幸福社會有愛

　　墻內墻外愛心牽繫

　　內修外行止於至善

　　的確真理發掘善根

　　十全十美難以圓滿

　　八分努力兩分助緣

　　盞盞明燈常在我心

　　燈燈點亮菩薩深耕

目次

第一盞心燈

監獄從來沒空過

教誨師不會失業，也不能休業
雖殘酷卻真實！
但我們感到更大的福分是
可以不停地為改善社會而努力
救一個人
其實也等於救了好幾個
承受悲歡離合的家庭
世上沒有絕望的處境
只有對處境絕望的人

林教誨師輕鬆地敘述：

有受刑人開玩笑地對我說：「我被判無期已關了十年，你們教誨師要關兩個無期以上，二十多年才可以退休，上班都關在一起，我們患難相依，有何不同？」

我解釋道：

「雖然在同一牆內，生活截然不同，我們進出自由，我們每天下班後，可以走出牆外與家人相聚，我們方向不同，我們除了修練自己，同時也要訓練大家早日悔改醒悟，能與別人和諧相處，你們則只要負責把自己內心的平衡力增強就好。」

他無可奈何說：

「在牆內我們有種種限制，不可能再變壞，也無理由來悍衛自己；那只鑰匙是掌握在你手裡，你們盡可高枕無憂了。」

「鑰匙雖是掌握在我們手裡，但命運是掌握在你們自己手中。」

我想轉變他的想法：

「對我們來說，我們的任務就是，要讓你們成為對社會有用之人，無論你們發生了什麼事，為了不讓你們對社會有敵意，我們得做好準備，除了設立宗教教誨的佛學會、慕道會、禱告會和讀書會等等之外，我們還要動腦設立各式各樣的藝文教育，藉由藝文的陶冶與藝術治療來柔化你們的性情，還要開設工廠讓你們學一技之長，好讓你們做好面對未來生活的準備。」我順便對他解釋我們的教育與任務。

「知道你們的好意。」他紅了眼眶繼續說。

「其實，並不完全是我的錯，才開始踏錯一步，就無法挽回，只能一路走下去，一路黑到這裡。」看來他似乎有點懊悔過去的行為。

我抓緊此刻鼓勵他說：

「現實是殘酷的，不能說是無辜，要勇敢面對脆弱的自己，我們都這麼努力在幫助你，你也要努力在每一個階段的課題做出決斷和保持意志力，每一次的決定，都要思考對於未來的後果是什麼，生活就是一場與自己的戰爭，沒有人可以不去面對，人生是很殘忍的，但命運還是可以掌握在自己手中。」

監獄與地獄只差一個字，但監獄從古至今一直都存在，而且從來沒有關閉過，因為人類的善與惡永遠都在拔河，謊言與真實的邊界，常常模糊難辨。每天都有人進出，所以教誨師不會失業。

但這是一份需要用不同的角度，細細深思的工作。因為關係到很多個人的權益，也關係到很多家庭的期待，還有更多人們的悲歡離合。做為一個教誨師，真的是身心備受煎熬，其辛苦自不待言。

世界各地有些地方的監獄，周圍環境優美，花草樹木皆照顧得井然有序，與古代的監獄，迥然不同。

現代受刑人的人道主義，也是氾濫成災，動不動就提出告訴，讓教誨師們戰戰兢兢，如臨深淵，如履薄冰，戒慎小心。

由於付出的心力和收入不成比例。因此教誨師若在職場的理念有更多宗教的耐心與愛心，與行善的概念，那就有無量功德了。

人們都曾有深感無能為力的時候，對於生活上的難題，無所適從，甚至於覺得孤掌難鳴，因此喜歡組織小團體，才不會淪為被孤立的個體，這樣的社會生活對於克服無能與自卑是有很大的助益。

在獄中，也要試著教他們培養幽默感，以幽默的眼光觀察事物，人世間處處有苦難，不如意事，十之八九，在獄所也能苦中作樂，即使一件極其瑣碎的小事，也可以引發莫大的喜悅，有人在獄中擬了一張快樂明細表，才發現還是有快樂的時光，與人互動合作，更有消愁破悶的忘憂時刻，因而增強了信心。

因人們沒有大猩猩、獅子、老虎般自我保護的本領，因此，無法獨自生存，需要社會生活。即使人們的喜怒哀樂，愛恨情仇，貪嗔痴疑，造成對他人的困擾，因而犯罪；但牢內大部分的人都是對他人、制度、社會規範等大都漠不關心的人。

因此教誨師除了品德教育外，還得要訓練他與他人和諧共存，對社會事務感興趣。

給多於取，多為別人設身處地想想，這樣地耕耘心地，也許無法短時間完成，但得堅持下去，因為——監獄從來沒有空過。

大家都活在同一片天空下，人其實並不孤單，也不用畏懼，只要擁有信任自己的力量。

「地獄不空，誓不成佛」。地藏王的悲心，可能就得從教誨師開始做起。

地藏王菩薩的悲願宏深，眾生度盡方證菩提，地獄未空誓不成佛，是我們要學習的使命。

地藏菩薩無數次地來五濁惡世救渡眾生，而眾生中最苦惱者是陷入地獄的眾生，所以地藏菩薩的悲願，就是從救拔地獄眾生起。

祝福人人心能淨化，諸惡莫作，眾善奉行。

誰沒有不懂事的時候，想一想，笑一笑

有人年輕時很嚮往過隱居山林的生活，沒想到，後來真的在偏僻的牢獄度日子，這不能怪老天多管閒事，因為機會總是留給有機會犯罪的人。

第二盞心燈

再見不是終點 ——
監獄是社會的縮影

人是隨著時間與不停選擇而轉向
且不斷變化終點的位置
而且有不一樣的代價
所以每個階段都要慎重選擇
更重要的是，應該要下定決心
選擇遠離的，是哪些道路

趙戒護科員看到不一樣的觀點：

監獄行刑法，第一條開宗明義，徒形拘役之執行，以使受刑人改悔向上，適於社會生活為目的，重塑人格，整裝再出發的所在。

很多人抨擊矯正署，說教化無用論，再犯率依然居高不下，毒品犯再犯率達七、八成，教化何用。坦白說，在高牆戒護的範圍裡，人就像當兵一樣戰戰兢兢，每日晨起做早操，但「退伍」之後，沒有約束了，還能遵守五點起床做早操嗎？

當我們接觸受刑人多了之後會發現：所謂善與惡的界限會越來越模糊，天使與惡魔也無法以二分法來劃界限。其實，監獄內就是小型社會的縮影。

有時候，我會覺得自己入錯行，因為在這個場域裡面，太多的悲歡離合，而讓自己不只心酸也沮喪。

幾年前，我曾經帶過受刑人返家奔喪，他因多次傷害人入監，他太太要來監獄見他，結果意外發生車禍，整個後腦勺都沒了……在殯儀館裡面，看到他太太整個後腦勺這樣泡在不鏽鋼托盤的血水裡面，頭髮也浮泛泡在血水裡！他看完之後，哭著跟我說，「怎麼辦？我覺得太對不起她！怎麼辦？已無法挽回了？」於是我跟他說：

「她用自己的生命來教育你，你也要痛定思痛，徹心改過，才能對得起她的生命。為她重新再作一位好父親，那才對得起她的犧牲。」後來就真的沒看到他再進來了，他已經改過向善了。

這是機會教育，這邊有太多的故事，讓人心痛。如果當時讓我再一次選擇職業，我要確定自己能夠承受得住這麼多的悲痛？因為這裡面有很多的真實人性，讓人扼腕。我覺得，這是要心智非常強壯的人，才能勝任的工作；要有一種任重道遠的精神，才能投入這份工作。

在高牆裡，沒有所謂的誘惑，只有愛心的老師，每個老師都很關心，很有使命，都很努力要幫助他們；而且在這環境內有一股約束力，受刑人就不得不改變。

但是當出獄後，誘惑、問題、考驗都來了，有沒有被貼標籤倒是其次，反而是生活、工作、家庭的問題，甚至親子、夫妻關係，都是需要重新磨合，重新溝通，一旦被困境打敗，身旁又無人提供協助支持，就會造成再犯率提高。再見不是不再見，出門後還會回來，而且一再重複！一般人的認知歸納這樣的結果，而得出教化無用論！事實上，我們提供的協助，是在受規範的時間與空間內，幫助受刑人除了反省與覺察自己的行為外，同時也教導增強抵抗外界誘惑的力量；期望他們出獄後能降低再犯率，回歸正常社會生活。但是人往往會輸給自己的習性，與牆外他人的影響。

所以說高牆內沒有壞人，教導做壞事的都是牆外的人噢！

受刑人大都活在自我為中心的世界，無法找到真正的勇

氣與自信，更無休戚與共的感受，身陷囹圄者，更應該要
學習樂於助人。

誰沒有不懂事的時候，想一想，笑一笑

有位 96 歲的老人，對年輕才 22 歲的警察說：警察叔叔，我要
報案，是誰偷走了我的歲月，還是時間總是在施工？

第三盞心燈

改變不能只說道理

童年遭受負面的影響

也許是一輩子的陰影

只有在成長過程中

自己努力重新建構目標與行為

才能改變

少年觀護所賴輔導員的體悟：

依法務部數字的統計，包含少觀所，受刑人來自經濟弱勢的家庭約占總數七、八成。通常犯罪的原因非常錯綜複雜，包含生理、心理、遺傳、家庭因素等等。依實務來講，原生家庭這一塊是影響最大的。一般的家庭，小孩子都會被悉心照料，但有些家裡顧不到的孩子就會四處遊蕩、或沒有錢去額外加強課業，最後成績落後，造成學習成就感低落，因課業跟不上而棄學；另外還有隔代教養、單親或新住民文化隔閡等問題。孩子的犯罪跟家庭環境有絕對關聯。

在整個社會氛圍下，少年觀護所的「住客」，明顯比較不受同情，因普遍認為凡是不良少年就把他關起來就好。

但在真正了解他們之後，會發現他們的生命故事，真是令人扼腕，甚至懷疑怎麼可能會有這樣的家庭！

到了少觀所，會發現這些小朋友們要的只是認同，所謂的認同就是你要把他當作是一般的孩子，你如果將他貼上不良標籤，他就會像拍皮球一樣，絕對彈得更高更遠，那我們就會如同在打地鼠一樣對之無法捉摸。然而，在少年觀護所愈久，就會愈帶愈高興，因為我們愈帶愈抓得到小朋友們的「眉角」；若覺得越來越好玩，他們就會越來越配合，其實，他們只是缺乏關愛的眼神。

有位朱老師，他剛來的時候，很令人擔心，因為太善良的老師都會被欺負，但他反而說小朋友都很乖，雖然班上有幾個確實較會起鬨，但同學們上他的課卻都像綿羊一樣乖順。因為朱老師是天主教徒，他有使命。

他認為：「上課時就把他們當成神的子民，也把他們當成羔羊，我是個牧人，所以他們再怎麼迷失他們的路，我都會把他們拉回來。」小朋友們反而覺得這老師很特別。

還有位牧師來上課，一開口就有位少年考他：「我們現在不是要上神愛世人的課嗎？那怎麼不唱神愛世人呢？」

牧師笑盈盈：「我們今天是為了慶祝母親節！我們要做十件讓媽媽高興的事情呀。」

牧師才講到第二件事，少年又說：「我們不是要唱神愛世人嗎？」

牧師說到第三件事，他就說老師可以了，我們來唱神愛世人。

牧師還是不厭其煩：「沒關係，等講到第四件事，我們就休息來唱神愛世人。」少年知道牧師喜歡唱神愛世人，他就是要看牧師的底線在哪裡。

牧師開始教作業了：「來，我們現在來畫卡片。」這位少年就是不理，可是牧師並沒有當場責難他，只是等待機會慢慢地跟他磨。

少年是混幫派，因殺人而進來。他爸爸中風後，沒辦法工作，媽媽在紡織工廠打工，可是入不敷出。他不是被家暴的小孩，可是他們家有土地糾紛，不曉得為什麼老是被欺負，從幼稚園開始他就知道拳頭可以解決問題，小時候，別人會丟石頭去他們家，他們的村莊整個家族都很瞧不起他們，後來家境好轉，他還是去幫忙討債公司，他說：「我在那裡有尊嚴，走路有風。」他認為在那邊有成就感，有認同感跟歸屬感。因為當時學校也不接納他。他入監後，很愛出風頭，卻會幫弱小的小朋友洗內褲。

牧師私下告訴我說：「我們只能用關愛的眼神，陪伴與支持，用時間來等待。因為只靠懲罰與責難並無法解決任何問題，若找不到真正的癥結所在，即使做再多的努力也是枉然。」

有一天，中風的爸爸坐著輪椅，讓媽媽推著進來，爸爸年紀很大，媽媽是外配，媽媽國語講得還不錯，也很關心他，可是少年卻很冷漠，我們趁此機會，讓他好好與父母親互動，結束時，我們還會要求小朋友們要抱抱爸爸媽媽：「感謝爸爸媽媽，今天對我們不離不棄，還來獄所看我們。」但我們發現這位少年很僵硬，他背對著父母，他不要說也不要做，這種情形在其他小朋友也是常見的，他是個典型，也是一個跡象。其實父母們都很關心，也都常來會面，但也許是緣於兒時經驗，或者關心與要求的方法，導致有錯誤的磨合，而此得到不如預期的回應。我們也只能溫和地，不斷地勸誡他，驅使他繼續前進，不要造成家人的負擔。

還有一位國小退休的老師，在女監輔導很久，她對輔導小朋友也很有興趣，可是小朋友會出作業考她，他們的態度是：「你們一定又有目的，反正你們說的都對，我們說得都是屎尿。」無論誰踩到那個地雷，他們就會為了反對而反對，他們絕對是在觀望你底線到底在哪裡。

剛開始，她快受不了，她說這比特殊教育班還難帶，不久來了一位過動兒，她找不到方法來糾正他，於是就耐心地教他書法，也許是感受到老師的關愛，三星期後，他居然會臨摹《心經》送給老師，而且從此以後表現頗佳，讓老師信心大增，終於體悟到，沒有教不好的學生，只有沒耐心的老師。

為人父母者，不知道也不願意承認自己的言行，造成了孩子今日的苦果，有時候，童年遭受負面的影響，若在成長過程中，沒有重新建構目標與行為療癒，早期經驗的創傷，可能就是一輩子的陰影。

誰沒有不懂事的時候，想一想，笑一笑

人不一定要會佛言佛語，也不一定要花言巧語，只要不胡言亂語就好，手語也是一種沉默的語言，只是不會生金，俗話說「沉默是金」。

第四盞心燈

孩子需要約束力與方向——
寵兒多不孝，嬌兒難成才

父母無法替孩子活出他們的人生
但必須肯定他的價值
幫助他在家裡找到歸屬感
父母的煩惱只會讓孩子腹背受敵

少年觀護所文輔導員的感嘆：

　　他從小就沒有母親，爸爸一直很辛苦地帶這孩子；可是卻很少給孩子約束力。爸爸很會賺錢，不斷地供給他錢；他在金錢取得容易之後，就開始方向走偏了。用錢來為所欲為地製造問題，如同他父親，供錢來解決孩子的問題。因此他從少年犯就進來監獄，久而久之，他已經完全適應監獄化生活，而在監獄內他可以被約束，很配合。可惜的是，他到外面在沒有約束力的情況下，就沒有辦法要求自己，也沒有辦法約束自己了。

　　他出獄後，我知道我跟他非親非故，我給他的約制力是很少、很小的，而且我們有時應該保持客觀，保持一點距離來看他所做的事情，遠遠地守護，不過度干預。後來，他就跟我失去連絡了，我找了他兩次，他都沒有回電，等到我再見到他的時候，他已經再次犯錯，又進來監獄了——二十七年的刑期！

看到他的樣子，我的感觸很深，他一輩子幾乎就要斷送在監獄裡面。他以前在所裡表現得很好，很聰明，會幫忙很多事，包括他的組長也對他讚譽有加。可是這麼好的人才，卻不斷在監獄裡面輪迴，令人惋惜，對他的家庭、對社會、對國家來講，都是浪費！

於是我找機會問他：「當你覺得你事情做得不對的時候，為什麼你才想到需要找我，是希望我能給你一點約制力，告訴你這樣做是不對的，是嗎？但是，你為什麼不學習給自己約束力？」他習慣了沒有約束自己的能力，更勝於察覺問題的能力。

除了學校教育，我一直覺得家庭教育和社會教育需要加強。其實，我們給學校的教育太多的期待了，期待學校能給孩子教到什麼程度？我常說，現在最糟糕的一個問題，就是很多家長會跟孩子講很多，跟社會講很多，可是當你到斑馬線前面的時候，你是否會越過那條「禁止線」？只為自己求方便，往往就把自己放大了。甚至於，有個犯偷竊的孩子，父親居然對孩子說，「你要文具，我可以從公司免費帶回來，你何需用偷的？」父親忘了，身教重於言教的古訓。

透過環境的學習跟模仿，在犯罪學裡面理論是成立的；環境的教育左右了他所學習的趨向。當家裡有客人來訪，若孩子端坐不動，我就會糾正孩子，「為什麼你沒有趕快站起來問候，而且是長輩來了。」他說現在的人都打成一片，我說我要打成兩片哩，我是長輩，阿姨、叔叔來，都是長輩，怎麼會跟年輕人打成一片，你要站起來，要問候。孩子有時候會反抗我們說管的太多，管得像人犯，但那卻是最基本的禮儀。

「看到長輩要站起來打招呼，你下次不這樣我會生氣。」因為他所接觸的一般同輩是這樣，所以習以為常就是這樣；但習以為常若是錯的，而不加糾正就是不對的！父母需要找出有效的方法引導他們，培養社會興趣外，進而與他人建立起共同感。心理學家阿德勒說，「個體心理學其實就是一門社會心理學。」

孩子並不完全是因為父母才變成這樣，雖然雙親對孩子的影響力很大，父母關切孩子的方式的確有需要改進的地方，但是父母不能為了改變孩子才改變自己。必須了解：即使改變自己，孩子可能會受到影響，也有可能無動於衷；父母的改變與孩子的改變，並無直接因果的關係。只有在父母是無所求的修，才有可能；孩子要不要改變，一切由他們自己決定。

我是一個在很嚴謹的家庭長大的孩子，我們家要做任何決定的時候，媽媽總是會提醒說，希望你眼光看遠一點，而無論什麼事情都要走向正途。

誰沒有不懂事的時候，想一想，笑一笑

如果您的兒子不懂事，請加入此群組，一起來探討與改善。加入後，也許會在群組裡發現，您父親也在。

第五盞心燈

自我超越是人類
存在的目標

無論處境多麼艱難

還是要抬頭看那陰霾的天空

找出隱藏的光芒

發心立願為人群服務

心靈就不會有瓶頸

虔誠懺悔，才能除去自我中心化

陳教誨師提醒生命珍貴的傳承：

有一位受刑人，他帶給我很大的遺憾，是性侵案。

他在家第一時間是選擇燒炭自殺，但沒有成功，進來後，我們有特別注意這個案。我曾陪他到醫院看診十四次，包含七次的外醫，感覺也有進步了，可是到最後，他還是自我放棄，他從不告訴任何人。他有任何的病痛，去做任何的移監檢查，都顯示是正常的。

可是突然有一天，還是不小心讓他自殺成功了！好難過！我很自責，因為這麼多的努力，他還是沒有自救，沒有超越自己的障礙。

最難過的是，他沒有對孩子們完成該交代的事，我認為他應該交予孩子一個正向的想法，雖然無法改變過去的慘痛經驗，也該讓孩子們知道今後該怎麼面對自己的人生，但他連說一句我知道做錯了！都沒有；他不僅沒有說半句道歉的話，還因走不出苦惱就選擇自我了斷，以為就此結束。殊不知，他會造成深遠的影響，他的孩子將無法學到如何超越錯誤的困境，而且這不只影響他的小孩，他的小孩會影響他的小小孩，最後會變成他是家族裡的創傷。

我一直很自責，覺得很對不起他的家人，雖然他的家人有來跟我道謝了，因為他們看過我們做了很多努力！

但我還是覺得，任何一個人的損失，我都會認為當初若能再多做些什麼就好。也許在這段期間應該投入更多的時間關懷他，好好勸他，才不會讓他欠了孩子一個交代。他的家庭 也因沒有爸爸這個角色，失去一半的親子關係了；我擔心他這樣行為的影響會更深遠！

生命的形式，不是只有一種，有可能是力量，也有可能因限制，而讓生命荒涼或孤寂，有些人自我監控的能力低，常以自我的情緒為中心來行動，因此容易違反社會默認的潛規則，導致傷害別人而不自知，淪落到入監服刑。

若能從新的觀點來看待自己的生命，改變自己的想法，就能從痛苦中解脫出來，周遭的人就會受到影響，只要不沉溺在悲傷中才會有力量。當遇到困難時，才學會做出相應的改變，而不是只選擇自我放棄。

　　因為，唯有從死亡的身上看不到成就感，只有無奈、無力、無助、與挫折感。

　　知道是自己的錯，無論是過去生，或年輕的時候犯的錯，沒有人能替他受苦或解除他的重荷，唯一的機運就是他承受痛苦的態度：向他們虔誠懺悔，請求他們原諒，把驕傲的頭低下來，誠心誠意地懺悔，並積極創造有價值與利他的事物，為自己的存在與尚待完成的工作，負起最大的責任。

　　祝福人人都知道悔改，虔誠懺悔，遠離絕境。

誰沒有不懂事的時候，想一想，笑一笑

有人去應試，居然考了零分，於是他仰天痛哭，「老天為什麼這樣對我？我又沒做錯什麼？」老天回答他說，你答錯了所有的題目。

第六盞心燈
善的使命以善養德

訓練人人都能與他人和諧共存
以克服自卑和不足
但一個人只有在無人監督的情況也能
堅持做正確的事
才算是真正成為自己的主人
這是獲得無悔人生必備的素質

周教化科長的行善使命：

坦白說，在這裡擔任公務人員要守住三個要件，才能夠平安到退休。第一是違法的事情不能做，非法的事情絕對不能做；第二是不安全的事情不能做；第三是不放心的事情不能做——就是說不能做主的事不能做。最基本的三個要件要掌握住，因為這都會影響到自己的未來，公務人員不能知法還犯法，明明知道不安全還做；除非有時事情是正面的，那就另當別論，只是伸張正義的時候要有法源依據，一定要是合法的，正義才能存在。

從前的父親都希望孩子們是公務員，因為是鐵飯碗，所以我們家裡的孩子多是公務人員，但唯一不是公務員的孩子收入最高，但我覺得自己快樂指數最高，因為可以不斷地幫助人。雖然學歷不代表能力，經歷不代表智慧，財力也不代表沒有壓力，犯罪也跟能力、財力都無關，但是我在這裡學到的人生經歷，就像是行善的使命，有機會幫助別人改惡向善，讓我覺得不虛度此生了。

雖然每個人都是一篇故事，但是每位受刑人，至少影響到三到五個的原生家庭──現有的家庭，包括太太那邊的家庭、還有被害人的家庭。每當看到他們懈怠偷懶時，我就會告誡他：

「你影響這麼大，你怎麼還有時間浪費！要趕快改變，對你的原生家庭，對你現有家庭，對受害者的家庭，你要改變，你的存在對他們、對社會才有意義，你才對得起天地萬物養活你。」

我們的功能，事實上，除了依法行政以外，只要能幫忙的，我們都會竭盡全力幫忙。因為這份工作，對他們的家裡，我們都是有責任的。但是今天若做了任何一個懲處，我會覺得只是將他與家庭拉得更遠而已。

從以前就覺得人已經變壞了，進到這裡面可能要花更多力氣去導正，不如在國中、高中以前，當孩子還好好的時候，多花一些時間在上面，不要讓他有機會變壞；他已經走偏了，要花很多時間來導正，真的很難。所以在可以被教育的時候，多投入一些資源在上面，總比已經變壞了，再要把他拉回來，要花更多的力氣好得多。希望政府在這方面能多多重視。如何預防孩子不要犯錯走偏，我建議從教科書著手，或設立更多讓他們發洩體力的場所，因為這跟家庭還有學校的環境太有關係了。

我常跟受刑人說：「當你每天夜深人靜的時候，想一想你思念的人；想一想你今天為什麼會在這裡？想一想，你要怎麼自我期許做一些改變。當你想完的時候，如果說你還有意志力的話，你把他記下來，把你人生最不快樂人生的這階段，做一些記錄，然後告訴自己說，再也不要走同樣的一段路。」

當他們在靜坐的時候，也會提醒他們，「其實你是能夠靜下心來的，尤其是你在監獄這段期間，是很辛苦的，你要深思為什麼我會把我的未來放在這個地方，我過去到底做錯了什麼？要能夠檢討、分析，尤其夜深人靜的時候，想想你的父母，想想家人，想想你所期待的人，你今天為什麼會在這裡？是因為過去做錯了什麼？希望你能真正的去回想，然後告訴自己不要再在這個地方輪迴。」

每當看到受刑人的改變，不再回流，對我來說就是最大的回饋了。

誰沒有不懂事的時候，想一想，笑一笑

有個小朋友的願望是，長大後要去當詐騙集團賺很多錢，然後去救濟窮人。老師說，這願望不錯，但是你要注意班上有好幾位同學，他們都說長大要當警察。

第七盞心燈

去感受別人心中的愛

相信每個人的本性是善良的
心中存有愛的
即使是惡魔，也有想表達的愛
只是他表達的方式
一般人無法接受
無法認可而已

賴藥師的慈悲之愛：

　有幾位同樣是受刑人的身分，平常除了幫忙清潔打掃之外，也會幫忙照顧一些病重的受刑人，需要管灌食的，幫忙擦澡洗澡的，上廁所，甚至於需要耐心地拉著人出來做復健。相信他們平常在家，都沒有這麼用心照顧自己的家人，這樣的行動，讓人很感動。定能讓自己與他人重新找回對於生命的希望與期盼。

　當他們在乎自己之餘，還能在獄中關懷他人，付出行動，定能逐漸解決生命中的問題。因為被關的不只你一個，當你關懷別人時，自己也得到安慰，周圍的人也會感染到人們溫情的善與愛。這樣的行為，讓我們都受到很大的鼓勵與感動。

因為人與人之間，有些相遇或相處，雖然注定不能長久，但只要有助人的行動，就會留下永恆的感動。

有時候錯，未必真正完全都是受刑人的錯；有的錯，是因他需要那樣的工作，但他們沒想到這樣會傷害別人，所以要給他們正確的目標，因為大部分的人都很自卑，都因承受不了壓力，而放棄脆弱的自己。

當接觸受刑人後，善惡會變得更模糊，因為他們在獄內的配合度，讓人超乎想像，比外面你我周遭同事，甚至更積極、更仔細、更耐心，更有愛心，會讓人懷疑，

這樣美好的人怎麼可能會犯法，或會犯錯呢？就像他們常常講的，拖鞋跟皮鞋之間，其實它的界線，就是一條線，只是那條線，有人踏過去，沒有被抓到，有人沒有踏過去，甚至有的人沒踏，只是因為法律嚴格的關係，他入罪了，他被判了刑了，在英文有句話說，你沒有犯法——直到你被抓到你才算犯法。

身體的病痛，在這裏一視同仁，這是醫護人員一貫的宗旨，受刑人是一個身份，不該成為唯一的標籤，全人類的

身體都是平等的，愛不分宗教、不分善惡，也是一律平等。

　　但其實醫護人員剛開始，也是抱著戰戰兢兢的心情進來的，戒慎恐懼，怕被他們兇，怕被他們挾持，或萬一對他們態度不好，出去後會不會被找麻煩等等。其實理解了他們所犯的罪刑其背後的陰影，就比較能夠同理。有人是一時衝動，有人是深根柢固的習慣，還有很多都是經濟弱勢家庭與單親家庭，或隔代教養長大的小孩，從小比較缺乏健全的愛，長大後，會有仇恨感，這也許是一種社會問題，也不完全是他們自己本身的錯。

　　其實這邊真的是可以看到人生百態，我也曾經看到受刑人，因為狀況已快不行而送去醫院，打電話給他兒子，他兒子竟然說，你不要再打來了，我去就是等領屍體。我說：你做晚輩的怎能這樣說！兒子說：他沒有盡到一些責任，所以我跟他不親，你要我把他帶回來，我這樣做就對得起我母親嗎？我只能安慰臨終的受刑人：

大哥，只能說你以前做得「太好」，你兒子現在才會這樣，你自己也要檢討，不能都怪你兒子。沒多久，他的兒子就真的來領遺體！

在這裏的生活，我們觀察到人心深處的隱祕，從這些隱祕中，窺知人性其實不過是善惡的混和，但善惡的分界線，每個情境不同，每個時刻不同，因人而異，因日而異，因時而異，只有內心最底層的愛是相同的。

造物者正俯視我們，祂一定不願意我們使祂失望，以相信世間有愛來感受愛，照顧病者，全部一視同仁。若能無所求付出愛，相信得到的大愛，一定會大於曾經付出的。

誰沒有不懂事的時候，想一想，笑一笑

你認為周圍的人都是垃圾，你就是垃圾桶；當你看到你的周圍，都是敵人要來攻擊你，你就已被敵人包圍了。如果你看到的人都是寶，你就是聚寶盒；當你看到周遭的人都是菩薩，你就是佛了。你的地位要件是取決於你的眼光。

第八盞心燈

有期待的目標，
意志力就會正增強

這世界充滿希望

學會樂觀，儲存正能量

只要找到活出意義的目標

意志力就會正增強

心中的燈泡亦能放大光明

林教誨師感染到的喜悅：

有位受刑人，從小父母都因吸毒而坐牢，他就像孤兒般長大，也從十幾歲被關到三十幾歲，出入監獄多次，我常教他要多看勵志的書，多儲存正能量，心想善意，才會有好事發生，眼看著他是逐日在進步了，果然，就有好事發生了。

有一天，他要假釋出獄了，他說有好消息要跟我說：「我女朋友要生孩子，我要跟她結婚了，雖然我已四十幾歲，剩餘的時間已不多，可是我從來就沒有家，但我會好好珍惜，不會讓孩子學我一樣，絕不會讓他成為孤兒。」他好像從沉睡中清醒過來一般，雙眼閃耀光芒，臉上洋溢著幸福感。

因為他在監獄表現良好，又有學習製麵的機會，所以出去會有工作，又可以娶老婆，要當爸爸了，真是有子萬事足，尤其他未來有固定的家需要負起責任，相信就可以增長他內在的力量，迎接人生的任務了。

聽到他的表白，我深深地感到欣慰，像獲得獎章般喜悅，後來他真的沒有再進來了，偶而還會打電話來與我問候。

每個人，人生的意義都不同，都得自行尋求，若找到了可堪期待未來的目標與責任，即使為之受盡屈辱，但內在的力量，仍會繼續增長。

家的支持很重要，有的監獄一年有幾次的懇親會，時間很短，有的監獄在懇親會之前，受刑人都要學習藝文表演，他們會讓家屬坐在最前面。

在家屬面前表演，得到的掌聲，也是很大的鼓勵，讓家人感覺你的進步，也讓受刑人感受到家人的支持，舉辦懇親會的意義會讓受刑人知道沒有被放棄，意志力會有正增強的制約學習。

對未來失去信心的受刑人，必然難逃劫數，一旦信念喪失，人格與精神防線亦告失守，接著，自然甘心沉淪。因為生命無論處在任何情況下，仍然都有其意義，這種無限的人生意義，涵蓋了痛苦和死亡，所以不能放棄希望，而失去了意義與尊嚴。

人只要活著，就有權利懷抱希望、健康、家庭、幸福、工作等等，這些都是可以重整旗鼓，東山再起的。過去不論經歷了什麼，也許都是未來的一筆資產，誰能預料未來會發生什麼重大的變化，畢竟連下一個鏡頭會有什麼變化，都沒人能預知，何況是未來？大好的時機，有時往往乍然降臨，也許就降臨在某些人身上，因為正能量強，好事真的就會發生了。

最讓我們感到鼓勵的，就是那句深刻銘心的話，「其實你救了一個人，也等於救了一個家庭。」我們其實是在救援家庭——讓當事人重生的家庭。

有人問證嚴法師，如何才能有意志力？

證嚴法師說：「你要問你自己，為何沒有意志力？」克服沒有能力的自卑感，還是得靠自己，不能把自己躲在舒適圈中，用白日夢來滿足優越感的假象。

誰沒有不懂事的時候，想一想，笑一笑

誰能想到，一場的偶遇，也許是這一生的奇遇，內在神性相互
連結，彼此靈魂有美好觸碰，那是幸運之神的降臨。

第九盞心燈

有勇氣走向有用之路

有時，人生在某個階段的選擇是錯的

而不自知

當初自認為有價值的東西

反而成了捆綁自己的枷鎖

要改變困境，唯有改變悲觀的性格

下定決心選擇一個重新生活的形態

更新道路

因為只有想不通不想改變的人

沒有走不通的路

劉教誨師鼓舞不同的信心：

　有位年輕女受刑人，她拒絕會見他的父母親，她只要她的男朋友，因為她從小父母離異，各自成家，她跟著奶奶一起生活，十五歲時奶奶過世，她靠救濟金過活。十七歲遇見男朋友，給她愛也給她毒品，於是她吸毒販毒，二十一歲入監，毒品與男友都是她溫暖與愛的象徵。但是男朋友自己也出入監獄多次，無法來探望她了。悲傷與孤單，讓她心情陷入低潮，自殘過好幾次。

　她訴苦說：「我也知道我要走好路，問題是我的好路在哪裡？我為什麼要走比別人難走的路，我有那麼笨嗎？我為什麼要去走那樣的路，不好的路我為什麼要走？如果你是我，那你告訴我，我的好路在哪裡？」

我也試著鼓勵她：「這條路妳既然都進來了，這正是改頭換面的好時機。沒人能幫妳承擔悲哀，妳總要學會自己長大，總要靠自己的力量堅強起來。我們最終都要為自己的選擇負起責任。」

後來我引領她加入工廠的烘培作業，學著在有益的面向磨練自己的心智，培養勇氣跨越自卑的情結，對自己愈來愈有信心了。

還有一位小朋友，童年的遭遇，迫使他經歷的，是一些不得不承受的痛，他對家裡是只有憎恨，再加一個冷漠，因為當年他媽媽離家出走，當他再去找到他媽媽的時候，他媽媽居然推說我已經另組家庭了，你不要再來打擾我，你這樣子讓我婆婆知道，我的婚姻會不幸福。小朋友是當場整個被拒絕，被遺棄了！當家人來會見時，他當然避不見面。

他的理由是：「你們是因為我被關了才要來關心我，你們是不是也覺得良心過意不去，才要來關心我？」這種感受確實是孩子行動背後的心理因素。他沒有體驗過同齡孩子的幸福家庭生活，他少了社會感，少了理解，少了勇氣，只有被遺棄的自卑情結陪他長大。

另外還有一位小朋友，他本身很有繪畫天分，但在十多歲就刺青混幫派，雖不是蓄意去殺人，但他在被判感化教育時，他媽媽自殺，除夕夜時在家裡自殺，在這期間，他爸爸還在混幫派。

他很心痛地打電話給我後，我馬上趕過去。

他說：「老師，你是我唯一的親人，我接連打了二十幾通電話，連我自己的家人都沒到，只有你到。」我很不捨地抱抱他，當然我也常鼓勵他要把絕望變成希望，讓他鼓起勇氣，聚積力量，畫出他有天分的特色，有勇氣走向有用之路來。

我們無法改變別人的命運，但可以轉變他們面對不可改變命運的態度，或在那一刻讓他了解痛苦的意義，目的在於獲得他們受苦的能力，勇敢接受苦難的挑戰，使自己還能工作與享受生命。

人生縱有千里江山可以行走，但能以利他的精神，走向有用之路，才能重新創造自己人生的故事。

誰沒有不懂事的時候，想一想，笑一笑

賣傘者的廣告：晴天八折，雨天九折，陰天請擦防曬霜，努力
賺錢買傘。

第十盞心燈
英雄難過心魔關

所有的英雄最終遇到的大魔王
就是自己的心魔
測量一個真正英雄的力量大小
應看他的自制力
不能克制自己，就永遠是個奴隸
能克制自己，才能駕馭自己
才是真英雄，能成就無限

林心理師認為最大的敵人是自己：

　根據法務部統計資料顯示，現在台灣因毒品入監的人數是二萬七千六百三十三人。毒品取得容易是一個問題，而且，不用很高昂的價錢就能拿到，剛開始他們是想要讓你上癮，等你上癮之後，他們馬上把價格飆高了，但還是得繼續吃下去。這問題實在是很無解，真的是很無解。毒品問題如果好解決，大概全世界每個國家不會把防制毒品，列為預算方面或是政治上面的問題了。

　有一位男吸毒者常訴說他以前的英勇，打敗過無數的敵手，連警察都畏懼他，但現在他居然拜倒在毒品的強勢下了。

　他辯解說，「不是我的錯，而是毒品太迷人了，以至於無法控制，無法抗拒，無法改變，而被打倒，你們為什麼要發明毒品，陷害我們入監？」於是我問他，「這麼說，無法控制，就表示這個下場，是你要的嗎？你也心甘情願，常住在這裡生活嗎？本來，目前的無法抗拒，就要在未來付出代價呀。」他無言，我繼續說：「不要把自己的欲求看得太重要，而失去未來，要為自己負責。來這裡就是要學習去掉自我中心，只要能戰勝自己，就沒有人或物能打倒你，你的心一旦放縱自己，就會被情緒和慾望的心魔牽制，就更不得自由。」

其實，被稱為意志薄弱的人，實際上經常比意志堅強的人，有更強的意志力，只是因為他們在生活上沒有確定的目標，他們要別人承擔責任，自己卻不負任何責任，還要享受別人創造的社會財富。

又有一位迷惑的毒男，他認為被關進來不合理：「我又沒殺人放火，也沒做什麼壞事，我只是吸毒，損壞的是我自己的身體，為什麼要把我關進來？」

「你吸的毒品，毒性強，不僅吸多了會讓你五臟六腑腐爛，還會失去人性，而任性傷害別人，危害社會，你自己不戒，是不想活了嗎？猶太教教義說，你若不為自己而活，還有誰要為你而活？一旦你失去人性，就沒有是非對錯的概念，只在乎自己的欲求，就會侵犯到別人，我們是要保護別人的呀。」我肯定地回答他的疑惑。

大部分神經質的人，總覺得只要自己本意善良，就能理直氣壯，但我們都知道，一個人如果只根據自己才懂的語言與道理行事，大都是精神官能症患者與罪犯，他們對於他人、制度、社會規範等等都漠不關心，他們的身心都在無用面向，只是想逃避，我們也有責任讓他們對於社會關懷感興趣。還要訓練他們增強心智力。因為佛經說：「若人欲了知，三世一切佛，一切唯心造。」《聖經》也說：「你要保守你的心，勝過保守一切，因為一生的果效，是由心發出。」愛因斯坦說：「瘋狂的是，我們在做同樣的事，一遍又一遍，但卻預期不同的結果。」

誰沒有不懂事的時候，想一想，笑一笑

他說他的存款有一億，最重要的是，那些錢是要用來治療他的
妄想症。

第十一盞心燈
孝順不能等

父母一生的辛苦和努力
都是為了給孩子更好的生活
為人子女要知恩、報恩

戒護科林專員說孝順的孩子才有福：

阿宏的母親八十多歲了，沒受過教育，每個月固定要給他三千元，每個月都來探監一次，車馬費起碼要花一千多塊，但他還一直要求買東買西，要母親再多寄一點錢給他，看得出來，這是個被寵壞的孩子，心裡裝的只有自己。

他還跟我抱怨說：「回家也不知要跟她說什麼，叫她來看我帶錢來就好，她總是帶了一些吃的用的，幹麼呀，真是氣不過，我把東西都丟給同學去吃了，這樣的母親完全不知怎麼溝通。」

我趕緊勸他：「因為媽媽在她那個年代原本就是這樣，她沒機會受好的教育，就只是把孩子拉拔長大，只管有沒有吃穿就好。你現在反過來指責父母親，這樣表示你雖然有受教育但也沒有學得很好呀，你如果受教育有學得好，就不會覺得媽媽這樣子是不對的，我們因為有受教育，所以可以跳脫出來看媽媽，知道媽媽是對的，因為她沒有受教育，應該是換我們來教她。何況，你媽媽花了多少心血把你養大，現在她年歲已大，你非但沒報答父母恩，還讓她擔憂，她還得從那麼遠的家鄉來探望你，你想一想，你忍心讓她還要擔憂你多久？你還有時間孝順她多久？不要等父母走了，才來後悔，那叫來不及的愛，那種後悔是一輩子都會痛。」他沉默許久。

「為了回饋母親的愛，你要痛定思痛，好好改過，重新做人，這也是你現在可以報答父母恩的唯一方法，錯過就來不及了。」

想不到，後來的懇親會，居然看到他抱住母親說感恩，不禁讓我也淚流滿眶。其實這份工作，讓我看到很多家庭的辛酸。我常看到家屬在外面徘徊，我心裡總覺得他們好辛苦！就為了見面三十分鐘。很多年邁的爸爸、媽媽拿著菜籃，千里迢迢，搭車排著隊來看小孩，拿的還不一定是孩子想要吃的，當然啦，這個跟孩子的爸爸、媽媽從小跟孩子的相處與溝通的教育問題很有關係。

我也曾看過，受刑人阿仁拿著菜籃到舍房直接就丟垃圾桶，我叫他過來，問他為什麼？他說，我叫他寄錢，他不給我寄錢，買這幹什麼？

我就直接勸他了：「你是男孩子，爸爸、媽媽生你下來，其實早期都很高興，生一個兒子可以幫忙工作；可是你有沒有想到？你不但沒有幫助家計，反而還多支出了一份，沒賺錢反而要開支。你有沒有想過呢？坊間流傳對於孩子的想法：「生個兒子，不如生個女兒，女兒還會庇蔭家裡；生一個兒子，對家裡不但沒幫助，有時還會製造麻煩，真的是這樣嗎？」這番話並不中聽，但我常常用它來激勵男受刑人，讓他們反思。

「那你還期待你爸爸、媽媽幫你做什麼嗎？你爸爸多辛苦！賺辛苦錢，還要幫你養小孩，還要每個月供應你三千元支用。你有想過那麼大的年紀，他是怎麼賺這些錢的嗎？」

後來不久，阿仁的媽媽往生了，我一路陪他，也跟他談一些人生的道理，還有讓他談他母親，他一談到母親的辛苦，情緒就控制不住，我記得非常清楚，早上六點帶他到高雄市立殯儀館，把母親遺體推出來時，他在他母親的遺體旁磕頭，一直磕頭一直磕頭，一直撞地上，跪著一直撞，用力撞，好像要用力撞破頭來表明他的悔恨，我把他扶起來規勸他，「雖然你現在沒辦法對你母親做什麼，我想你是不是就念佛，迴向給你母親，你還要下定決心改變，才能安撫她在天之靈。」 我在那邊陪他一個半小時，我自己也買一些糖果餅乾，讓他就跪在那邊祭拜母親。

後來，所裡有人對執行懲罰有怨言時，阿仁會仗義直言規勸他們，「這個主任其實是一位面惡心善，有仁慈心的人，曾經幫我不少忙。」也許是他的規勸而平息了犯責房的紛爭。

就算是有一兩千位受刑人，我只要能拉到一兩位悔悟過來，我就覺得一切的辛苦都值得了。

今年，我感覺老天也幫我很大的忙，我得了猛爆性肝炎，我住院才十四天就出來了，那天有位師姊到我家，跟我媽說，妳兒子真的有修到功德，有辦法兩個禮拜就痊癒出院，讓我感覺我真的是要認真再繼續走這一條路，有能力就多作一點，雖然身在公門，可能有些受刑人他的行為有點偏差，我還是要糾正，當然當下他們會反彈，或有負面的想法，但是我覺得與人相處久了就知道，要用愛溝通，我都跟我老媽說，心存善念那就 OK。

因為我以前也是外婆把我帶大的，我哥哥是我奶奶帶的，我們沒有隔代教養的問題，只要有感恩心，要知恩報恩，老天不會虧待有厚道的人。

其實在這裡看了很多人，然後也讓自己常去審視自己，對自己家人有沒有更貼心？對自己家人真的做到了嗎？也盡全力去做好自己該做的工作了嗎？

誰沒有不懂事的時候，想一想，笑一笑

選擇等待的位置很重要，在不對的地方，永遠不可能等到，就像在公車站等捷運，在機場等候一艘船，有人笑說，您是在等飛船嗎？

第十二盞心燈

貪汙與犯罪都是
學習而來的

貪汙犯罪，都是學習來的

不好的習慣也是累積而來的

多閱讀

古人說「書讀百遍，其義自見」

反覆閱讀，可以從中獲得新的信心

人總是太容易因為別人的一言一語而失去信心

克服恐懼與焦慮是人生學習的目標

李政風室主任提醒教育才能匡正偏差思維：

我覺得貪汙犯罪，都是學習來的，那些不好的習慣也是累積而來的，每天上班都跟他們關在一起，要管理他們真的要有一套，我們比較有資源，所以你要求別人對你有向心力，不是要求對方先配合你，你才去釋出善意，而是擁有資源的我們，先釋出善意，盡量地幫忙他，自然他就會順應。相信在一般公司，對待員工也是一樣，這應該就是鐵律。

專員有很多種，有的是以預防為取向，你快要跌倒了，趕快把你拉一把；有的人是等你跌倒再拉你；也不能說什麼是對，什麼是不對。如果想要立功就等事情爆發，平日發呆什麼都不管，等到事情發生再做，有許多公務員是這樣子，但是我相信只要是做對的事就好，一旦你跨過紅線，儘管我沒什麼權限，那就移送地檢署，送廉政署辦理，法院若願意判你無罪，那是你的命，不是我的責任。但是只要讓我知道你越了紅線，很抱歉我有職責要執行，因為這是國家賦與我的責任。

這邊的主管與管理者本身都是「白色」，但每天與形形色色的受刑人，接觸久了就變了，想法會改變，人會變，也會影響他的家庭。所以我們得時時內省，正視當前處境的嚴肅性與尊嚴，因為老天也正俯視我們的工作，他一定不願意我們讓祂失望。就是這樣，人要畫一條紅線，你管教受刑人，如果能讓他們棄惡揚善，並能為社會所用為目的，這才是我們本分的工作，要常提醒自己這份工作的重要性，但是不能超越公務人員應有的理性，有時候很難，因為在不斷接觸的過程裡，這條線不斷在移動，你會覺得受刑人的生活，跟你的生活幾乎是一致的，很難劃分，如何切出一條分際線來，上班是上班，下班是下班，你該過公務員應過的生活，這最難。

因為在幫助受刑人中，有時會陷入一種複雜而微妙的悲憫之情，最難把握的是適當地釋出，不會讓人引起貪念的善意，要常常提醒自己，有些原則，對我們是多麼重要，需要審思與學習。

　　所以人人需要驅使自己有學習的欲望，接受教育，譬如有一群流氓，儘管體力很好，但關鍵在於教育，如果教的好，就可以當羅賓漢，把他們的榮譽感激發出來，當然要激發他們的過程是很辛苦，特種部隊不是人人都可以生存下來的。

　　像台灣很多小朋友沉迷電玩遊戲中的血腥殺戮，有些遊戲都殺得轟轟烈烈，小朋友學到的是遇到敵手，殺無赦，但人生不只是一場遊戲，永遠都有敵手要克服，到哪裡都會有朋友，到哪裡也會有敵人，有時候朋友會變敵人，所以人際關係的溝通是很迫切地需要學習。

　　只要是人，就一定會透過情緒感受來合理化自己的態度，可能在這裡看得比較多，相對的對自己的小孩子要求比較不嚴苛，但我教育孩子們從小要有正確的觀念，我尊重天地君親師，絕不准孩子直呼我名字，一定要稱爸爸媽媽，如果叫我名字我會糾正他。中國人就是中國人，你基本的禮貌一定要有，那是傳統文化教育的最後一道防線，也是現代學校體制應該發展的方向，因為法律只是治標不治本。

有許多家長給予孩子的壓力很大，孩子會自暴自棄，或是反彈，或背離父母，誤入歧途，所以小孩偶而犯錯，第一次會原諒；沒有人不犯錯，第一次犯錯當然要講一下，重複犯錯當然就不可以，或者只會看到他們做的是否違反法律，不會像其他家長要求那麼多。今天你不乖只要求不要變壞，成績次要，等他沒有變壞比較正常，你就會要求他的成績了，不讀書當然要盡量鼓勵，但不讀也沒辦法，人的品德最重要，不可以打罵人，欺負弱小。當孩子身體不健康躺在病床上，你什麼東西都不會計較了，只會要求病趕快好，等身體健康了，就會要求其他，多學習多做好事，盡能力就有意想不到的收獲，這就是人生。

書看得越多，越有收獲，雖說接觸信仰是在培養信心，但是沒有碰到困難就不會去拜佛，讀了《正信的佛教》那本書之後，我改變了，心越來越柔軟，像我從小練拳練得極好，但從不打人，我卻曾被抗告方圍毆，打得很慘，差點沒命。我是做對的事，所以老天待我不薄，讓我活出更健壯的身體，感覺手腳更有力了。但以前軍官都說，「武士不濫殺無辜會有報應，武士更不可以被濫殺，這是尊嚴問題。」

而今學會遇到難題，心還是可以柔軟的。證嚴法師說：「能原諒別人才能善待自己。」你生病了，就能體會生病時的痛，不經一事不長一智，真的就是這樣。我已學會了逗大家笑，我覺得能帶給人家歡笑是一種福氣。

有些受刑人必須經過不斷的教導，才能學習到一個平凡的事實；沒有人有權做壞事，即使受欺凌的人亦然，更應學習的是，在獲釋之後，回歸故里時，面對親友異樣眼神的心理準備，也許會受不了幻滅打擊而消沉頹喪，難再振作，甚至於產生憤怒而精神失調，即使心理醫師有時候也難以幫助他們克服這一層心理障礙。還有必須要再重新慢慢學習的是，感受快樂的能力，那是幸福的智慧，因為快樂是可以學習的。

　　大家都在期待受刑人能夠改邪歸正，回歸正常的生活，那也是我們的目標。

誰沒有不懂事的時候，想一想，笑一笑

悲劇是，雖學會了一身的功力，卻不知如何下手，但最最大的悲劇是下了手卻傷了不該傷的人。

第十三盞心燈

別在傷口上撒鹽

人不需要因喪失身體的自由而愁苦
而是要善用珍貴的心靈資產
讓負面思考轉為正向
用利他的角度來深思人性

林社工師談人是需要多鼓勵少揭傷疤：

這位少觀所的小朋友是第三次進來，進來的時候哭得唏哩嘩啦，十七歲第三次進來，第一次進來是十四歲，原因是毒品，十六歲進來時也是因為毒品。他一直擺脫不了毒品問題，直到後來，他已經從吸食「進階」到販賣！因為沒錢，就加入幫派。

其實不管他的家庭因素怎麼樣，判決書就已經寫的非常清楚，只要我們不要一天到晚問他：你犯什麼罪？你是因為什麼罪進來？這對他們來說都是一個傷害，因為那就像標籤一樣，永遠搓不掉。

他已經跟大人一樣，從警察局到地檢署到法院，到判刑去執行科報到要發監，發監又來收容，都是在問他犯什麼罪？為什麼？……可是一再的要他回答，這對同學來講是一種傷害，不可承擔的重量。

在傷口上灑鹽，是二度傷害，要他面對他所犯的錯，有些人會覺得說，我已經面對一次了，再一次，第三次，第四次，到後來，他們會感到自卑沒自信，對人產生不信任感，接下來會想放棄自己，就爛到底了，我出去，再回來就好啦。

我們處理小朋友暴行打架，我不會先問他，你為什麼打人？我們會先處理他的情緒，今天到底怎麼了？等他情緒真的穩定，他反而會跟你說打人的理由。

有一個小朋友說，加入幫派，是因為他家遭到別人丟石頭破壞，他們身上其實都有強大的自卑情結。因莽撞、傲慢而好勝，我們會發現，他們永遠都想超越自身的能力，脾氣不好的孩子，常會借著出其不意的攻擊來控制他人，他們為何毫無耐性呢，因為他們感到自卑，覺得自己不夠好，不夠強，而他們也渴望能夠克服這種情結，於是用最容易的打人方式來獲得成就、尊嚴與優越感。

我們必須找到適當的方法來治療這些孩子，因為他們沒有發現生命的整體性，也不知道事物的自然順序，我們不能指責，也不能質疑，因為他們要能夠更堅持自己才不會自卑。因此，只能以和善的態度向他們解釋我們的觀點，讓他們了解自己問題的所在。並且多多鼓勵他們學會幫助別人。

人們在內心受傷，懷抱不安的時候，難免會壓抑情緒，以免他人察覺，就算已經痛苦得想大哭一場，但言行舉止仍然力圖冷靜，這不一定是刻意要裝酷耍帥，有時只是壓抑情緒而已，許多面無表情的人，內心深處其實都承受著深層的陰影。

其實每一個人都有自卑感，但自卑不是疾病，而是激勵人們以健康的態度，來延伸出向上發展的力量，但只要一切努力是為了追求對社會人類有用的事物，價值觀就不會偏差，而犯罪大都始於價值觀的偏差。

如果有人問，文明社會中最強大者是誰？答案是嬰兒，因為他們完全不受他人控制，是真正的王者。

祝福人人在每一個逆境中，都能歡喜心接受，並能穿越苦難。

誰沒有不懂事的時候，想一想，笑一笑

人世間哭笑不得的事雖多，莫過於心裏的石頭落了地，卻砸到自己的腳，而傷痛了心。

第十四盞心燈

只在乎自己無法
適應社會

我們屬於我們所生存的這個世界
自己並非世界中心
只在乎自己的利益得失者
就沒有適應社會的能力
很難成為有用之人

吳教誨師提及無奈的案例：

　　從小就不乖的豫宏，父親的個性極火爆，常把他吊起來打，打到半死，父母親沒有離婚，現在已是高齡。他二十幾年來，大部分時間都是獨居，因為他沒辦法跟別人相處，會打架，不太想工作，他已經被關了二十多年。

　　豫宏已離婚，一個兒子，據他所述以前自己的成就還滿好的，因為我們要提報假釋，三十年前就有規定，長刑期戶籍要遷到監獄裏面，現在，我們提報假釋是出去要有固定居住所，要家人提供入住同意書，跟戶口名簿，他父親一直不肯，對他很失望，因為他對誰都提告，他跟他父親要錢，要他寄幾千塊錢，他父親不肯，他就告他父親侵占，他說他之前留有一部車子，現在要使用，又說什麼他老婆偷領了他郵局裏的錢，他也要提告等等。這種人格是違常的，他只對自己有興趣，只在乎自己的利益得失，沒辦法按照常理來管教他，他從十多年前過來開始，他是在我的教區，我們互動都算不錯，他有些文具、電話卡，因為沒有人給錢，都是我提供，還有一台收音機的電池也是我提供給他，因他沒錢買。但差不多半年前，因為做輔導紀錄，我寫的紀錄讓他簽名，多聊幾句，前面那一段當天做的輔導，寫的時候沒有帶上去，他就把我以前對他的好處，完全否定掉，而且還告我在裏面怎樣使壞害他，到後來，我們全部都被他亂告。

一般的受刑人都很感恩教誨師。現在的受刑人，因有了人權保護，動不動就要告監獄人員，以前監獄比較封閉，我們要做任何事，只要是對的就可以去做，比較沒有顧忌，現在到處都有監視器，我們要做的事，一切都得按規定來，不然很容易就挨告。

但為了他要假釋但沒有地址，我跟他父親聯絡，他父親很明確地說，他們家族一致通過，不希望他回來，我也打電話給他兒子，他兒子卻提出質疑，「你看我爸爸這樣有改過嗎？可以通過假釋嗎？」而且他已結婚家中有新生兒，也不希望他回來打亂了家庭生活，我們請他們提供戶籍入住同意書，他父親多填一個字「入住不同意書」，裏面還註記誰放誰負責，家裏的管道沒了。我也曾經跟一位牧師安排與他談話，牧師以前也被關過，同意要幫忙，結果回去三天後，我再跟他聯繫時，牧師回去網路一看，他們也不同意了。本來要提供後續追蹤用地址，沒人願意承擔了，可是沒有地址就無法執行保護管束，假釋有一條規定，假釋必須有固定居住所，固定正當職業。如果地址是在宜蘭要到宜蘭地檢署報到，剛開始兩個禮拜報到一次，後來正常可能一個月，後來三個月等等，所以一定要有地址。

其實要他有正常工作，也是不容易。今天願意提供十個或二十個這樣的機會給這些受刑人，自己要先把標籤淡化掉，這是很基本的心理建設。企業主自己也要知道他的過去，如果真正接納他之後，不能把它變成未來跟企業主之間的問題。他也很難找到沒有頂頭上司的工作，或不用團隊的工作，有鑑於他只在乎自己的利益得失，無法與周遭人建立好的關係，這樣的人並不是值得信賴的工作或事業夥伴，因他永遠都將個人利益擺在公司整體利益之上。這樣的人，在職涯上往往不是勝利組，不去找目標追尋，而只在怕吃虧的妄想中，是無法讓地獄變天堂。

 **誰沒有不懂事的時候，想一想，笑一笑**

有些人做錯了事，絕不承認自己有錯，只會說自己很辛苦，這樣的人，可能會一輩子辛苦下去了。

第十五盞心燈

刻痕的標記——刺青

每一次困境都是療癒的開始
也是成長的開始
重要的是要找回人格主導權
面對他人的期待時
藉由什麼來證明自己
而不會失去未來

少年觀護所鍾輔導員訴說接納：

要全然接納更生人，真不容易，但就像接納顏面燒燙傷的人，不能有優越的情結，也必須要有面對有殘缺的人的勇氣，這輔導的工作，就是要能全然接納，因為這是要用心的專業，這絕對不是只有愛心而已，因為考慮不周全的愛心也會讓他們再次受到傷害。這樣直截了當的拒絕，是給他二度的傷害。

有位少觀所出來的少年朋友他，他請我幫忙找工作，我介紹一位老師，她曾信誓旦旦說要幫他找更好的工作，於是帶他去看這位老師，老師被他的刺青嚇壞了，當面跟他說刺青先處理完，再來找我，少年人很傷心，從此他也就不再跟我聯絡了，當時我也受到很大的挫折與傷害。

有一次我試問另一位刺青的少年，他說這不可能洗掉啦！「老師我不會去除刺青，我跟它相依為命，我從十一歲開始進幫派，每一點都是我發洩心情的時候刻的，是我心情沮喪的時候刻的，每個印記都是我的成長過程，是我生活的一部分，也是我生命的故事，我不可能把以前記憶一次抹煞，老師，我會面對我的生命，我不管別人怎麼看我，我就是我。」

　　這個少年朋友說要為自己負責的話，讓我很震撼，他全身可能要花一百萬去除掉全身的刺青，他不是因為怕花錢，或怕痛拒絕，他只是勇敢說出了他生命的祕密。

　　我們不需要給他們任何判斷，因為事實上，真理會自然呈現，年輕人自行決定願意為自己負責，是很負責任的事。但最重要的是，他用什麼樣的態度來詮釋他的生命。

　　刺青算是一個標誌，可是社會風氣，仍然將刺青視為叛逆等負面形象，有些年輕人很容易一時性起，去模仿偶像的烙印，而忽略了會帶給自己的形象負面的效果。

　　近年來，「悔青」的青年人數愈來愈多，但衍生的相關費用也很大，雖然有醫院與公益團體已開放了一些免費名額。

因為台灣的幫派刺青，有很多喜歡刺鬼頭、刺龍，刺鳳，這跟美國文化不一樣，甚至於說刺一個鬼王，有位宗教方面的老師還說，那是代表菩薩的化身。刺青的目的，有的是顯示自己的歸屬，以幫派的小朋友而言，他加入幫派，為了身分地位，會嘗試刺青，沒有刺青好像永遠是小弟；譬如說暴力討債，一群人出去，五十個人，最後面的弟弟可能領八百，站在前面的，可能兩千、五千的，按照階級，算是地位的象徵。

小朋友在剛加入幫派的時候，要的是一個所謂的歸屬感和成就感，因為在學校他格格不入，他功課不好，可能在家，也都是被父母責備，怎麼不去念書，怎麼考那麼爛？在學校也是，人家都在拚會考、拚考試，只有他一人閒閒無事，因為功課跟不上，有的老師還不錯，會讓小朋友趴在桌上，可是有的同學會認為，你這樣帶壞我們班上風氣，就會排擠他。

這些小朋友去哪裡可以相濡以沫，去哪邊可以找到同病相憐的同伴呢，最後就會加入幫派了！

誰沒有不懂事的時候，想一想，笑一笑

有一位看手相面相的算命師，掛的招牌寫著，這是個看臉看手的社會。

第十六盞心燈

放下自己的志工精神

不怕不進步，只怕不起步

人類的愛是有限，會用盡

無私的愛需要以志工的精神培養

關注他人勝於自己

以小愛化大愛

陳行政輔導員的生命就是志工精神：

　　在這個環境工作將近二十八年了，自己也成長很多，以前長官給的任務，我很少沒有完成，大部分會超前，不會辜負他們所託，他們給我一個綽號叫使命必達。然後六年前，冷不防地一個早晨，他們叫我去蓋個章，我被調動了，看不出來我接到訊息當天是想吐的，因為換了個新任務，好像廢了我所有的武功，雖然一樣在管理受刑人，環境也駕輕就熟，但到了這個區塊變成新生兒，我所有東西都歸零，面對很多人事物都頓生無力感，我在裡面只能努力掙扎，一個月後會務還不能跟上，電腦操作也不熟悉，很多東西都得重新學習，我只好連續三年每年都請同仁吃一桌，因為需要聯繫感情，需要別人的鼓勵。

剛開始到這裡真的很憂鬱，一直覺得被廢了武功，都處在負面的情緒中，後來我嘗試去懇親會主持節目，辦活動拿麥克風，做機關的導覽，還有學習進退應對跟著別人做事，其實這樣反而讓我學得更多，因為那樣角度就不是局限在只跟著受刑人，我的觸角更廣寬，在那裏面讓我改變最大的是看到志工的柔軟，當然很多都是退休老師，還有是社會上有名望的人進來當志工，尤其是慈濟的志工，看到他們的謙遜跟縮小自己，我以前認為自己已做得很好，自大跟狂妄，認為自己很重要，與志工們對比之下讓我羞愧，看見人家那麼有實力，還縮得那麼小，那麼謙虛，我們拿薪水是不是要更積極，志工們是付出無所求，還甘願做眾生的貴人，以菩薩的心，照顧眾生，在人群中自動自發服務奉獻，這點鼓勵了我產生積極去應對更多事情，到現在我認為工作上沒接觸過的，反而可以重新再學習，應該要感恩，轉念之後，我察覺到自己以前個性上的迷思，知道要感恩知足，內心找回了熱忱，已沒有缺口了，其他都是多餘的。

我們這麼多年的管理跟教化，跟受刑人比較熟悉，一般外面的志工進到我們的系統比較陌生，還要適應，他們也不知道受刑人的需求，我盡可能幫助他們，為了讓自己更好，我還參加弟子規種子教師培訓，也修了茶藝師證照，就想要教他們弟子規正統的禮儀，孩子們習氣雖不同，也許可以替媽媽們要求這些孩子坐要怎麼坐，聽課要如何專注，進退應對要有禮貌，因為我們教誨師們都好忙，想為他們設計一個道統禮儀，把它當成我們家孩子犯錯，代替媽媽來糾正做一個規範。

　　我曾經遇到同學在舍房過度換氣，應該是氣喘，但是他是屬於過度換氣，同學反映說他死了，記得受訓時說處理速度要快，急救的東西都要做出來，要鎮定，接著是人若死了，要開始勘驗、保存證據等問題。那天我是加班，就很鎮定跟同學說，不要慌不要怕，把人給送出來就好，還記得那時候前面一排舍房門全部人都在看我處理，在人生中面對受刑人往生是很大的災難，然後我把門打開，就開始做 CPR 了，人拖出來臉是黑的，不知道是否休克，但一個人也沒辦法呼救，找人撥電話找護士，護士還在那一頭，黃金急救是幾分鐘而已，我就一直做 CPR，跟他口對口人工呼吸，一直做一直做，心想即使死了也是要做，因為這是我的職責，做到護士來接手，還開始要做一連串的聯繫工作。

到第二天，人犯居然坐在我面前，鼻涕還是流著，我跟他說，你這個樣子我昨天還是跟你口對口人工呼吸哪，你還真的活過來了，很感恩喔，還記得那件事長官記了我兩支嘉獎，當然嘉獎的鼓勵比不上他活過來的意義，更讓我有了成就感的獎勵。後來回想當時也不怕他有沒有愛滋病等，反正救人第一。現在的 CPR 不需要口對口的人工呼吸，是直接心臟按摩就可以，但人犯是死的，我人卻是緊張的，那種狀況是我比較難忘的。

另外有社會背景的老大姐，到監所裡面來，可能由於情緒非常的混亂，在舍房裡面會敲門會攻擊監視器潑水潑糞，什麼狀況都有，她說是被冤枉，我們都會說妳就依程序來，台灣是三審定案，你可以請律師抗告、訴願、訴訟……可以提出有力證據，我們用盡了種種輔導方法，她就是不聽，到最後她還是寫信給總統府，給壹週刊，也寫給她要求援的部分，說她是被冤枉。

受刑人進來不管有沒有受冤枉，但若一直不承認這個官司的時候，他是會發瘋的，他的行為幾乎是瘋狂的，通常男受刑人，兩千多人中會十個類似像這樣的狀況，不平不滿在醫學上我們會說他是憂鬱症、躁鬱症，不會說是瘋子，但他的行為我們看了是瘋了，他做出許多的行為，近乎瘋的階段，所以他除了沒有死之外他什麼都會做，他會攻擊人，會踢門，也會找事跟人挑戰，那是躁，有一種則是一直想死，那是鬱，你會以為他是個違規者，其實他面對這樣生活環境，還有他的官司，他認為生存是無希望的，我們對於他搗亂的行為，除了生活管理要加強警戒之外，還需有心靈志工的輔導，再來就是投藥治療，同時安排親人的撫慰，這四個面向同時進行輔導。受刑人在這裡不能把他當作瘋子，除了關好顧好一直做警戒，擔心他一死了之，光這樣是不夠的，一定要四個面向馬上執行，他那個瘋狂程度，就像個超級大瘋子。我們管理人員和教誨師的比例，相對於受刑人都是相當不足的，如何對待他們情緒的治療，是需要很大的耐心跟人力的資源，每座監獄大約有兩千多個男受刑人，要去對付其中最難搞的十個，真的需要很大的耐力 。

後來我接觸到佛教，佛經有教義，《聖經》也有教義，都有很好的警世語言來啟迪我們，我們用這些話來撫平我們內心的不安，我曾帶同學念佛號，抄經文，那一刻，我覺得世間好祥和。我相信信仰能使人和諧共處。因為有宗教信仰的人比較不會焦慮。誠如證嚴法師所說，宗教是生命的宗旨，生活的教化。

誰沒有不懂事的時候，想一想，笑一笑

既然上班不開心，為什麼還要去上班？不為什麼，只為下班就很開心，當志工更開心。

第十七盞心燈

一勤天下無難事

理不在懂不懂，只在做不做

天道酬勤，地道酬善

改變生活形態，才能改變行為

改變就從勤勞作業開始！

詹作業科長對勤奮有獨到見解：

　勤奮的人，沒有時間養出壞習慣，許多受刑人皆以自我
為中心的導向，他們追逐的是虛假的目標，過的是無用的
人生觀。要讓生命改變，第一個就是從外打破，第二個就
是從內打破，作業就是要讓他們勞動，勞動就能從外打破
他自己，養成勤勞的習慣，從內打破就是重生，去掉自我
為中心，訓練每個人都能與他人和諧共存，彼此感恩。

　達文西說：「鐵無用則鏽蝕，水若停滯則不再純淨，且
會在天冷時凍結，人若無為，就會弱化心靈的活力。」

　但在監內是一定要作業的，這是立法規定的，再來就是
要技能訓練，就是讓他們在獄中，學有一技之長，出去之
後真的可以學以致用，跟社會的脈動潮流能夠結合，學習

配合大家的作業，也就是去掉自我中心。

　　法令有規定，在四種情況下不需作業，譬如例假日是不能作業，還有他的直系血親往生了，要讓他安靜，不能強迫他作業，再來是罹病，不然就是正在戒護跟教化中。

　　慈濟志工定期來教導蔬食料理，尤其在女監，從不會拿菜刀能獨當一面，她們的廚藝有餐廳級水準，更開辦有烘焙班，有受刑人出獄後，來信感恩說已開了饅頭店，生意特佳，可以謀生了。讀信之後，我們感受到很大的鼓勵。

　　我們是以現實的趨勢來規劃這一部份，第一個一定是要符合當地較本有的技術或是傳統工業，還是一些可能會瀕臨失傳，或比較夯的行業；比較不要求太高深的技術，只要肯用點腦筋，就學會的，像是腳底按摩，就是最近很夯的；大家都講求養生的推拿按摩，除了學得一技之長，還可以在家幫父母與家人服務，療癒親情的疏離。此外，更設計了混和當地技術與傳統技藝，有擔心技藝會失傳的，或行業本身不會衰退的，譬如木工班即是。就讓收容人在這裡，如何有創意地去運用。但必須要選擇受刑人，因場地受限，且被招訓的人須是在一年內即將要出監所的。

　　以前都說拜師學藝要三年，但我們必須在一年內把功夫學好。縱使不懂，只要有興趣又能夠專心投入的話，一年應該是夠的。我們的訓練班一期是三個月，兩期就是六個月，比如烘焙班，我們有六個老師，每個老師學到兩招就好了，六個人有十二招，就可以養活自己了。學完出去之後不會忘記，讓他有興趣並保持住那一股衝勁，出去之後真的是可以謀生，因為沒有工作，再犯率一定是非常高。刑期判很久的人，當然對他也不能夠失去公平，他們也會在工廠作業，只要身體健康，還是要做電子零件加工，折紙袋、紙蓮花等等都有讓他們勞動到。

　　如果，本身有特殊才能，而且他刑期很長，我們會有自營作業，讓他能夠學以致用，讓他在這個地方能夠發揮他的創意跟技術功夫等等，我們當然會特別處理，但這樣的人才真的不多，我們會用所謂的專案，專簽的方式給他遷過來，好好讓他在這邊創造一些產值。

　　在裡面有些同學跟你非常的配合，即使有些人的配合未必出自內心，但「假久也會成真」，但也有可能是個性關係，有人做事就是認真，或因為法律有假釋制度，為了趕快有假釋機會，所以不得不跟獄方配合。但是毒品犯會比較狡猾，因為他習慣的環境讓他學會見風轉舵，他知道要討好誰，可以有不勞而獲的方法。說謊變成一種生活習慣，他從頭到尾都會一直編故事給你聽，講到後來，才願意投入作業，努力工作直到最後一班，流過汗後，發現他可以開始講實話了。

生命來來往往，有長刑期有短刑期，沒有來日方長，只有努力工作，過日子減生命，生活安穩，四肢健全的人，更應該要好好把握，充分發揮生命的良能，才對得起天地雨露，滋養我們。

誰沒有不懂事的時候，想一想，笑一笑

不想做，不願意去做，安於現狀以為是與世無爭，承受不了一點壓力，只想不勞而獲，就像溫水煮青蛙，這種人是舒服死的。

第十八盞心燈

在被安置之處播種光

真正的邪惡
是靈魂的冷漠
有感恩心
才體會得到光的溫暖

謝典獄長的熱忱是因為感恩：

　我是較偏向於經營管理，怎樣把一個監獄，人與事的環境都發揮最高的效益，是我最喜歡做的事。這十幾年來，無論是被調到哪個監獄，每一個階段我都要找出自己的熱忱與創意，相信生命都有其意義，最需要是靠自己努力播種。因為在一個監獄，就是這些人、這些經費，如何把它做最好的運用，讓受刑人看見光明，對明天有多一點美好的感覺。

　教育是需要言教、身教、還有境教，如同山谷裡的松樹與山頂上的松樹，樹種雖同，成長環境不同，就會呈現不同的生命型態，所以環境的教育，會左右人們成長的趨向。

監獄是一所閉關的學校，老師們的職責是在訓練受刑人，能在艱苦多難中站起來，境教很重要，裡面生活待遇稍微好一點，舒服一點，就能感覺世間的美好，讓他出去對明天還抱著希望，讓照顧他們的員工，工作上更有成就感，不會是每個月領薪水過日子，整個監獄每個月都要讓它進步。

第一次住進金門時，曾經嘗試改善他們的作業，從本來的摺金紙，摺紙蓮花，到串水晶吊飾，讓受刑人收入增加十倍，讓我信心大增，因為這樣就不用再讓受刑家人接濟了。也請人來教作金門麵線，又開發了紅蘿蔔麵線、紅麴麵線、甚至於菠菜麵線，銷路很不錯，大家都做得笑哈哈，現在金門麵線，一年賣一千萬，真的是不可思議。

可是有位來教導的老師，卻困惑地說，「你讓他們學，學成之後出去要跟我們拚生意是嗎？」

每個人的立場不同，有不同的想法，是理所當然，「因有您們的功夫，還有您們發心的功德，他們才有機會學習，學功夫也是一門學問，也許以前他有潛能但沒有機會，他們不是要搶做生意，您們是在教他們技術，希望將來能有一技之長，雖然是學到您們的一點點功力，但還不知他們將來能否做成生意，用賺錢為誘因更能激發出興趣，這對他們往後的人生，是非常有價值的，他們能因此增強信心，也許就能回歸社會成為有用之人，社會若少一些犯罪的人，這社會就多一份安和不是嗎？您們的功德真是無量。」

有位受刑人寫信給我，「很感恩，我領到作業基金，除了賠償外，今年我寄了一些錢回家給孩子念書了。」我離開金門後，陸續收到許多感恩信，他們感受到我的努力，但該感謝的是整個團隊的盡心盡力，還有老天給我的空間，可以做很多事，這樣的感恩沖散了人與人之間不順暢的苦惱，也支撐著我，繼續往前努力。

因為我學過空間改善，也在另一個監獄，花很少的經費，以八個月的時間擴廠完成，讓醬油產量增加，有些受刑人領到錢，他們說可以償還被害人的補償，與自己的生活經費了。讓我感到很欣慰。

當在南部監獄時，天氣很熱，一直思索，應該來做太陽能發電，於是請他們趕緊收集資料，然後標來建置，規劃一年要保障多少度的發電，發電賣給台電，有多少收益。我們的建置，其實是不用花錢的，每天發電，賣的錢，雖然爭取給我們的所，但會計法規說不行，這錢要全繳國庫。

總務科長埋怨了：「賺的錢我們所裡又收不到，幹麼要這麼辛苦？」

但我認為還是要堅持，「有兩個理由，一定要做，第一，賺了錢是給國庫，也是我們的國家。第二，我們是要替他們降低溫度，屋頂都是平頂，陽光一照射，真的很熱，晚上他們回到房間，那個熱氣逼下來，是會受不了，將心比心，感同身受，我們還是要做。」

我調職離開後不久，聽說他們已開始在運作發電，而且已能發電一萬度了，他們來電，盼望啟用時我能去，我說，不用！不用！你們自己去弄就好！反正，成效能留在大家的心裡，覺得做對了一件事就可以了。

這次又到了不一樣的監獄，看到我們的懇親宿舍還有役男的宿舍，我跟科室主管說，你們小孩如果住這樣的地方，你們難道都沒意見？這邊環境怎麼會這麼爛，窗子沒有窗簾都貼報紙，床鋪爛得缺角，職員的宿舍也是，以前新科員來報到，看一看，他們都寧可去外面租房子，不住了。於是我就動手，改善環境，因為讓空間潔淨通風，才能清除內心汙濁的空氣，窗戶明亮，才看得見光，才能留得住員工。我每天跟我太太下了班，就繞著圍牆走，看看還有什麼需要改善的。

心靈的環境，也要加強，慈濟香積團隊過來，教他們煮蔬食料理，尊重生命，愛地球，這才發現這裡女生都不會做菜，還有生命教育的讀書會，書法班，更生人講座等等，更有演繹《父母恩重難報經》，讓許多受刑人痛哭懺悔自己的錯誤，這些都是在加強受刑人改邪歸正的動力與勇氣。

但我家不是有錢人，所以凡事都斤斤計較，在監獄裡該省的我會把預算抓得很緊。連以前買原子筆也是，一次兩百打、三百打，一、兩個月就買一次，他們說，每個月固定發一次。我認為不妥，一支原子筆，每天寫，可以寫兩到三個月，他們上夜班簽一下到，怎麼每個月要一枝？不可以這樣，該省的連這小錢也要省下來。

無論調到哪一個單位，我都用感恩的心承接下來，努力播種光，然後用笑臉對待被離棄的人，幫助他們聽到自己良知的呼喚。

其實，沒有一帆風順的人生，年輕時有一個階段，一直在追逐名位，常怨老天不公平，我每天很認真埋頭苦幹工作，可是升官還是沒希望，很懊惱，其實，我從來也沒有跟長官要求，我要哪一個位置？我想調去哪裡？可是長官們怎麼沒看到我每天這麼忙，這麼認真做，沒獎勵，不僅沒升遷，反而被調到比原來更小的單位！當時我一兩個月都輾轉難眠，派遣的那個晚上，我沒睡，端坐沉思，又沒犯錯，怎麼會這麼不合情理，後來看到窗外，月亮無私地照耀大地，轉念勸自己「力惡其不出於身也，不必為己」，能受天磨，方成鐵漢，相信長官們，一定有不得已的苦衷，何必為難長官。證嚴法師也說：「人生不一定球球是好球，但是有歷練的強打者，隨時都可以揮棒。」如此一想，自己就從心裡微笑起來。

「謝謝長官給我方便，讓我不用搬家搬很遠。」第二天一早特地去見長官，我用體諒的笑容，感恩的話語，他很驚訝，稱許地點點頭。我認為做該做的事，做就對了，何必計較官位大小，當找到感恩之處，心靈已感受到光輝，但還是很感謝自己，能夠做一個改變觀點的人。

很多事也讓我學習忍耐，有時候科長講很不像樣的話，我也忍下來，從不罵人，所以我的孫女說，阿公你脾氣很好，我跟孫女說，不好聽的話，就當做沒聽到就好，她若跟弟弟吵架，也是這樣教她，不好聽的話，當做他在念經，沒聽到，別理他就好了。睡個覺起來，明天還有別的事要做，就把它淡忘了。

有一位鄰居跟我說：「我好羨慕您喔，您在這個位置，可以做這麼多事，我寧可少活五年，來跟您換這個位置。」真的，我一直都很感恩至今的福澤，很感恩這些年來，我能在被安置的地方，努力開花，播種希望的光明。很多事情是要靠自己積極行動才有成就。我們隨時可以退休，重要的是即使上了年紀，還是可以抱著能為別人做些什麼的心，相信這樣能帶來生活的力量與勇氣。

因為，一生所留下來的，不是我們獲得的東西，而是我們所付出給予的。

誰沒有不懂事的時候，想一想，笑一笑

發脾氣是虧本的一種生意，受到侮辱要當作是培養福氣；這道理還不錯，可是有些人發怒上癮了，說白了那是「轉」大人，沒轉過，就是長期性的短暫發瘋。

後記

讓心念轉向正向能量

在我們的生命之火，即將黯淡奄奄一息的時候，有人吹上一口氣，使光焰重現，我們會懷抱最深的感謝，如同有些觀念，點燃我們內心的電光石火，讓我們轉念，讓我們歡喜，讓我們感恩，但能否讓念頭延續不滅，還是得靠自己的努力。

曾聽到一位法師，回答一位生了智障兒的母親說：我寧願相信，您的孩子是菩薩，他是來替眾生承擔苦難的。當下的觀點讓那母親轉念釋然了。

為什麼有人一出生就處於淚水與苦難中，有時候，受害人往往會變成加害人，甚至也是暴力循環的受害者， 因為接受到的訊息，只有用暴力才能解決問題，為了保護自己，只有用暴力來對付，因為他沒有學會其他的方法因應。有時候，必須在情緒上，審視自己，找出為什麼會做的理由，犯罪大都始於觀念的偏差。

曾經在一場導讀會上，分享精神病患的笑話，希望能博君一笑，想讓氣氛輕鬆，沒想到，會後有位聽眾過來提醒我，「您知道精神病患的家屬，多麼痛苦嗎？他們的日子過得多艱難嗎？」當下，我非常懺悔，沒有去同理周圍家屬們的感受，趕緊合掌感恩他的提醒，我們往往都沒去感受病患背後親人的立場，他們的笑話講一次只有三分鐘，但家屬們，卻是天天時時刻刻都必須生活在哭笑不得，憂心忡忡的世界裡。

由此聯想到受刑人，他們的背後，承受悲歡離合的家屬。因為如同書中的案例，「如果我們也經歷這樣的事，旁邊的情況會怎樣？」因為紀錄他們對受刑人的教誨，從此，我也學會了退一步多觀察，多敞開心胸來旁觀周圍人的感受，如同從別人的立場來看自己，是否更有慈悲與憐憫之心。

監獄內的教誨師們與各科主管們，他們殷殷期待社會能改變得更祥和，所以花了不少心力，希望促進受刑人的心理健康，讓他們更有仁慈心，重新以不同的方式，跟自己與跟他人和諧相處，找出解決問題的方法，修復補償被害人與其家人衍生的悲痛，也對他人有所貢獻。像是高牆內的路燈，照亮路也照亮人心，讓他們看到方向。

古代刑法處罰犯罪行為，講求隔離主義及應報主義，但在大約自一九七○年代中葉開始，一些司法人員和被害者團體開始注意到被害人於傳統的刑事訴訟中，不被重視的境況，只是個被傳喚來作證的證人。為了促使被害人及其家屬的傷痛被國家重視，為了讓犯人認識他造成怎樣的傷害，給犯人道歉或彌補的機會，所以在加拿大、紐西蘭等地開始仿傚當地原住民的風俗，試行修復式正義。

關於「修復式正義」，維基百科的解釋大抵為：關於修復式正義（Restorative Justice，或譯：修復式司法）基於「和平創建」（peace-making）的思維，主張處理犯罪事件不應只從法律觀點，而也應從「社會衝突」、「人際關係間的衝突」觀點來解決犯罪事件。強調「社會關係」的修復，亦即，當事者的權利、尊嚴應得到滿足，個人、團體與社區已損壞的關係亦得到應有的修復。換言之，社會復歸不只加害人，連同被害者及社區均需復歸的刑事政策理念——在國家制度保障下，透過任一方都不吃虧的程序，讓各方當事人早日回歸正常生活。執行修復式正義時必須避免強迫或誘騙被害者，以廉價條件原諒加害者，也要避免加害者假裝改過；尤在性侵殺人虐待等無法或難以回復的犯罪（這類犯罪容易讓受害者或其家人有嚴重心理疾病，這種病是難以治癒及控制的，病人會承受終身痛苦），修復式正義更要謹慎使用，尤其是必須正視被害者與家屬的受害嚴重性，否則修復式正義會成為對受害者的嘲諷、重罪輕判的藉口、對犯罪的鼓勵及吃案的同義詞。

非常感恩此書的紀錄出版，沈慈夷師姐與楊濟昶師兄的導引與一路陪伴，還有陳秀琇師姐的鼓勵，劉慈柔師姐的支持，在此深致感恩！更感恩監獄裏典獄長與各科室主管們的接受訪問，才能將此書順利出版。此書的版稅將捐給宜蘭監獄，作為回饋他們對受刑人的用心與教誨。

殷切盼望高牆內與牆外的人，因閱讀此書，更能體會大家的期盼，而善自珍重，把軟弱的時刻與暗彈的淚水，化為勇氣，超越困境，找出生存的目的與責任感，因而活出生命的使命。

證嚴法師說：提燈照路，是一種光明的象徵，希望人人不只在元宵節提燈，要永遠點燃智慧之燈，不只自照心路，且能燈燈相傳，照亮人人心的道路。

Contents

Introduction

Seeing Light in the Darkest Nights

For the world travelers, someone returning home from an island vacation was about to get mugged by an armed robber but somehow was saved and able to go home safely. Another person who mistook a bag of powder purportedly as a gift at the airport ended up in prison and risked losing everything in life.

This world is filled with miraculous and incredible events, and our life, impermanent and fleeting, is constantly being tested by choices and judgment calls–what to do and what not to do, what brings good or bad results–something that seems good now may turn out bad later. However, there will be unavoidable situations and unforgiving fate from which we cannot escape. We need to persevere until the very end to attain the most satisfactory outcome and realize its innermost teaching. The most important factor will be the attitude we adopt when faced with adversity and our competency to handle it with equanimity and assertiveness.

Dharma Master Cheng Yen says, "Adversity only comes by chance; do not waste the opportunity." If we meet all the challenges with poise and serenity supported by our religious beliefs and inspired by the wonders of nature such as a flower, a tree, or a glimpse of sun at dusk or dawn, we shall find consolation. Nietzsche said, "He who has a why to live can bear almost any how."

Even when one is confined behind the high walls, so long as he is aware of his mistakes and able to muster the willpower to begin his life again, he can always aspire to great things that have a noble end; he will possess the resolve to face all the challenges ahead as well as transforming the guilt and pain in him into glimmers of hope.

One day, my friends and I went to a prison doing book donation, and when we got to the front entrance, my friend telephoned me to see where I was. "In prison," I absent-mindedly answered. "What! What happened to you?" She screamed with so much shock one would think I had dropped down to hell.

When we were about to leave, another friend called, "Where are you now?" "I am just leaving prison!" There was a pause, then, gingerly, she said, "So, no more trouble with you, right?"

Prison, with its high walls, is sealed off from the outside world; it is a place where the criminals pay their dues with their freedom. Whenever we speak of the prison, there is always a feeling of dread and mystery.

However, inmates may not realize all the efforts the counselors and supervisors put in to rehabilitate them. With wisdom and compassion, they tirelessly employ different ways to help the inmates see where they had gone wrong, and learn to choose between right and wrong by appealing to their innate nature of empathy. This way, they will not be lured by temptations once released from the prison and will stay out of trouble as well as re-entering the society as a productive member. Within the high walls, the counselors are like the beacons of light that brightens the dark corners of the inmates' hearts.

On this earth, no one is an island; we are all interconnected, and each of our choices will invariably have an effect on other people. Any emotional upheavals or subtle mood changes will give rise to the so-called butterfly effects. Owing to this phenomenon, we are all somewhat responsible for everything that has been happening. By deciding to do everything with loving kindness, we will somehow create circles of virtue, for peace and happiness are possible only if the rest of the world has them, too.

I would like to thank all the counselors and supervisors who allowed me to document their acts of compassion in words. Ebbs and flows of remorse and sadness filled the pages of the interviews as untold secrets buried deep down inside the inmates' heart convulse and burst with raging furies. The counselors are sometimes like a Bodhisattva with his gentle gaze and infinite compassion, but are at times like a wrathful deity with his majestic ferocity. It is not possible to stay out as a bystander. They radiate light of loving kindness to quench their afflictions. Over the course of many years, they have been relentless in teaching the inmates by words and by skillful means, hoping that some of them might be reformed. That will be their greatest reward, for their greatest aspiration is freeing them of suffering.

It is my hope that the stories in this book will inspire you to look beyond the superficiality of this mundane world and get a glimpse of its complexity and profundity. Know that this world does not revolve around you. It does not matter if you are weak or strong; so long as you do not set a limit on yourself, we all have the potential and responsibility to do our part to make this world a better place.

Here, let us bring all "Eighteen Lamps Behind The High Walls" to light, and dust off life's afflictions. I hope at least one of the lamps will brighten not only your heart but also that of everyone else. It is my earnest wish the lamps will also illuminate the love outside the walls and make this world bright with radiance.

Let's turn the light on.

Please remove the light cover, and dust off all the afflictions in your heart.

Heart Lamp #1

This Prison Will Never Be Empty

Lesson: The harsh reality of being a prison counselor is that we will never be out of work or off duty. We are doubly blessed to be doing our part for the greater good of society. When we save one soul, we also save the many suffering families interconnected with that person.

A prison counselor, Mr. Lin, recounted his stories with a light heart:

An inmate once joked, "I've already served the first 10 years of my life sentence, but it seems you are serving two life sentences with 20 more years to go until you retire. You are stuck with me day after day. What is the difference between you and me?" I replied, "Within these walls, we are still living two very different lives. I get to move about freely and see my family after work. I am always learning ways to do my job better to help you do the right things and reconnect with the community. Your only job is to regain your lost inner peace."

He was nonchalant, "I am watched so closely here I can't do anything bad anyway. You are holding all the cards. You get to sleep like a baby at night." I explained to him, "Yes, I've got the key to your cell, but you still hold the key to your future. My job is to help you become a productive member of society, and not one who looks at it as an enemy. We have Buddhist and Christian study groups as well as art and cultural classes that are designed to tame your mind. We also have career training to give you the job skills you will need later on in life."

He looked sullen, "I see what you're trying to do for me. Actually, it wasn't all my fault. After my first run-in with the law, I just started sliding down a slippery slope until I ended up here." Sensing some regret in him, I added, "Yes, reality is harsh. You need the courage to own up to your mistakes. We are all here trying to help you, and you need to be strong at heart and stay the course. Think about the consequences of every action you take. The battle you fight in life is always with yourself. Everyone has to face their own enemy. Life can be cruel, but you can still be in charge of your destiny."

The Chinese words for hell and prison differ only by one character, but prison has been around since ancient times, and has never been out of business due to the perennial tug-of-war between good and evil. The distinction between truth and falsehood is blurring. There are constant new arrivals to the prison, providing job security for the counselors. However, their job requires in-depth thinking about the inmates on many different levels, such as their civil rights, their families' expectations, and all the emotional baggage that comes with their incarceration. It can be a daunting and thankless job.

There are also prisons in other parts of the world that look like resorts with manicured landscapes, quite the opposite of the olden days. Their prisoners' tendency for human rights lawsuits is also becoming pervasive, instilling fear in the hearts of counselors for any perceived legal wrongdoing.

It would really behoove the counselors to have some religious moral support such as patience, love, and a general desire to do good because their pay is just not commensurate with the amount of work they have to put into their job.

Everyone can feel powerless at times, unable to cope with life's challenges, and feel quite lonely. This is the reason individuals want to form groups, so they do not end up feeling isolated. Groups can really benefit those with poor social skills and low self-esteem.

Human beings lack the survival skills that animals such as monkeys, tigers or panthers have. We cannot live alone, and need a community. However, people can succumb to greed, passion, aggression and end up committing crimes. Those who are behind bars tend to have a general disregard for other people and social mores.

A prison counselor should not only give inmates a character education, but also teach them how to coexist with people and invest in their community. They should learn to give more and take less, and to take an interest in other people's welfare. All this may not happen right away, and will take time, but we must persevere. This is the reason that prisons will never be empty.

Ksitigarbha Bodhisattva vowed to not attain buddhahood so long as there is one soul left in the hell realm. A prison counselor should embrace the same mission and be inspired by his vast and profound compassionate vow. He came to our world of Five Turbidities to save us, especially beings who are suffering the most the hell realm, and will not wish to enter enlightenment so long as there is even one soul left in the hell realm.

Please keep your sense of humor when reading the following. Smile. Everyone messes up sometimes.

There was a person who had always wanted to retire in a secluded place. To his surprise, he actually ended up in a secluded prison. You cannot blame heaven for having a hand in this; opportunities are reserved for those who take advantage of them.

Heart Lamp #2

Good-bye is Not the End, Prison as a Microcosm of Society

Lesson: People change with time, with the choices they make, and with different outcomes in life. This is the reason we need to choose wisely, but more importantly, choose which paths not to take.

From the correction officer Mr. Zhao's point of view:

Enforcement Rules of the Prison Serving Act clearly states in its first articles that prisoner's interests shall be taken into consideration when prison officials perform their duties.

Many people criticize the Agency of Corrections for being ineffective in bringing down crime rates while the drug rehab relapse rate hovers around 70-80%. To be sure, within the confines of prison walls, life is rigid, like in the military, where everyone gets up early doing exercise drills. Once they are released, will they continue getting up at five and do the same?

The more inmates I know, the more I feel the differences between good and evil are not so clear-cut, just as the differences between angels and devils are not so black-and-white anymore. A prison, in reality, is a smaller version of society. At times, I wonder if I have chosen the wrong profession, for I have seen too many heartrending stories of human travail. These really saddened and discouraged me.

Several years ago, I took an inmate, who had been in and out of prison many times for assault, home for his wife's funeral. His wife had been on her way to visit him when she got into a fatal car crash. At the mortuary, he saw half of her skull missing, only a metal bracket holding her blood-soaked head and hair. After seeing her like that, he was heart-broken, "What can I do now? This is all my fault! What now? It is all too late now." I told him, "Your wife gave up her life in order to give you this lesson, and you need to take away something from this pain. Be a changed man. This is how you can repay her life. Be a good father so that her sacrifice will not have been in vain." After that, I actually never saw him back in prison. He was a totally changed man.

This was a case of situational learning, of which there are many heartbreaking stories. As a counselor, if I could choose my profession again, how would I be sure that I could take all this emotional toll? There is so much raw humanity that makes us shudder. My feeling is that to excel at this job requires people with a strong mental constitution and a sense of purpose and destiny.

Within these walls, one will find no so-called indulgences, only deeply-caring counselors with loving hearts and a mission to help. The inmates cannot help but change in this disciplined environment.

However, once inmates get out, many temptations and headaches will once again test their wills. Social stigma being the least of their concerns, they have to worry about re-entering society, finding jobs, reconnecting with their families and dealing with their spouses and children, all big challenges to overcome. The recidivism rate is high among those who have no social network for support and are not able to cope with the challenges of re-entering society. Farewell is not good-bye when the same people continue to be put back in prison. In a nutshell, this is the argument for the ineffectiveness of the correctional system. Actually, we not only try to help inmates reform while they are locked up in prison, but we also try to inoculate them against evil influences once they get out. Our aim is to reduce their recidivism rate so they can live a normal life. However, old habits die hard. The people with whom they hang out after their release are also a major influence.

We can even postulate that there are no bad people inside prison walls; all evil influences can only be found outside of the walls!

Most inmates tend to have a self-centered view on life, and have very little courage or self-esteem. They lack altruism and the ability to empathize with other people. While in prison, it is even more important for them to learn the meaning of helping others.

Please keep your sense of humor when reading the following. Smile. Everyone messes up sometimes.

A 96-year-old man tells a 22-year-old police officer, "Officer, I want to file a Missing Years report. Someone stole all my years. Could it be time that has been working me over?"

Heart Lamp #3

Words Will Not Bring Real Changes

Lesson: Negative childhood experiences can cast long shadows over one's life. As one ages, only by assiduously adopting new goals and behavior can one hope for changes.

From juvenile detention center counselor Mr. Lai:

According to the Ministry of Justice, of all people incarcerated, including juveniles, 70-80% come from economically disadvantaged families. While the causes of crime are complex—involving biology, psychology, genetic, family of origin and other factors—in reality, the family factor is the most influential. In a normal family, the kids enjoy being at the center of attention, but in others, kids may be neglected and left to wonder around aimlessly. Some families do not have the resources necessary to help their children learn, which can result in poor performance at school and feeling inferior and ultimately quitting school. Additionally, there are challenges such as skipped-generational rearing, single-parenting and foreign spouse cultural disparity issues. single parents, and cultural gaps and frictions with foreign spouses. There is a definite link between juvenile delinquency and family unit structure.

Juvenile detention centers often do not get much sympathy from the public at large. People tend to think of them as young thugs who deserve to be locked up. On closer examination, though, one may find their stories heartrending and wonder how families such as these could even exist.

At detention centers, one thing all children crave is approval. They all want to be treated like normal kids. Once they are labeled as criminals, the result will be like hitting a ball hard and having it bounce high and far away. As it turns out, the more time we spend with them, the more joy we feel from them. We begin to understand them more intimately. The more fun we have with them, the better their behavior becomes. They are merely deprived of love.

When Mr. Zhu, a new counselor, came to the detention

center, we were concerned because he was too nice. The kids tend to pick on the nice ones. However, it turned out all the kids were quite obedient despite a few troublemakers. They were as tame as lambs. Mr. Zhu is a Catholic on a mission.

He said, "These are God's people in my classroom, my flock of sheep, and I am the shepherd who will guide them, however astray they may have gone." In this way, the kids found their teacher quite special.

And then there was another counselor, a priest, who was teased by one of the students, "I thought we were going to learn how much God loves this world. Why aren't we singing 'For God So Loves the World' yet?"

The priest smiled, "Today is Mother's Day, so we are going to list ten things that make our mothers happy."

The priest had barely got to the second item when the kid interrupted, "Why aren't we singing 'For God So Loves the World'?"

When he got to the third item the kid interrupted again, saying enough was enough, and it was time to sing.

The priest was undeterred, "Sure, no problem. Let's finish the fourth thing on the list, and then we will take a break and sing." The kid knew the minister loved the song, and was testing to see where the priest's bottom line was.

As the kids were doing class work, the priest said, "Now let's draw a card." One kid acted as if he did not hear him, but the priest did not discipline him. He was waiting for the right moment to change him.

The kid was in gangs, and was imprisoned for manslaughter. His father could not work after a stroke, and the money his mother earned from working at a textile factory barely made ends meet. He was not an abused child, but due to a land dispute, his family was somehow continually harassed. Since kindergarten, he only knew how to deal with problems with his fists. People used to throw rocks at his house, and all his relatives in the village looked down on his family. Even after his family became better off, he was still working as a debt collector for the mob. He recalled, "Everyone respected me. I was walking on air." He felt a sense of accomplishment and belonging. His school did not want to have anything to do with him. He liked strutting around in prison, but would befriend the weak ones and show camaraderie by washing underwear together.

The priest confided in me, "We can only watch over him with love, companionship and support, and just let time do its work because punishment and reprimands alone will not solve any problems. If we cannot get to the root of his issues, then however much effort we put in will still be of no use."

One day, his stroke-ridden father came in to see him with his mother pushing the wheelchair. He was already quite old, and the mother, despite being a foreign bride, could speak decent Mandarin Chinese. She was quite worried about him, but the youngster was cold to her.

I had wanted the visit to be an opportunity for them to spend time together as a family. Before it was over, I asked him, and all other kids having family meetings, to hug their parents and tell them, "Thank you, Mom and Dad, for not quitting on me and for coming back to see me." This kid, however, was stiff and turned his back on his parents, not wanting to say or do anything, —a reaction quite typical of other kids, too. It is a sign. The fact is that all parents cared a great deal about their children and came to visit them quite often. Maybe it was the overbearing way that they had been raised that led to their antagonism, which their parents had not expected. All we can do is guide children with compassion and patience so that they do not end up being a burden to their families.

There was also a retired elementary school teacher with extensive experience counseling inmates at women's prisons who became interested in and started working with juvenile delinquents. However, the kids kept trying her patience, saying, "You are up to something. We don't care what you say because whatever you say is holy and whatever we say is shit." It was like stepping on a landmine; the kids will defy her just for the sake of it. They wanted to see where her bottom line was.

At first, she could not stand it, saying that it was actually harder than teaching a special education class. Soon after, there was a hyperactive kid whom she was trying to help. Not being able to find the right approach, she resorted to teaching him calligraphy. Perhaps her tireless effort led him to feel that she actually cared, and as a result the kid was able to produce a copy of the Heart Sutra within three weeks and gave it to her as a gift. She was elated. After that the kid continued to make steady progress. Finally, she realized that if there is a problem in the classroom, the reason is not that the children are unable to learn, but that the teachers are too impatient to spend the time teaching.

Parents are either unaware or unwilling to admit that they are the ones who gave their children misguided bad influences. Negative childhood experiences can often linger on throughout developing years. If they are not able to begin healing with new goals and behavioral changes, those early childhood traumatic experiences will cast inexorable shadows over their lives as well as inflicting devastating wounds on society.

Please keep your sense of humor when reading the following. Smile. Everyone messes up sometimes.

We do not need to parrot the Buddha's teachings, or use honeyed words; we just need to not talk nonsense. Sign language is a language of silence, but it will not bear gold as in the proverb, "Silence is golden."

Heart Lamp #4

A Child Needs Discipline and Guidance. Spoiled Children Will Not Love Their Parents and or Lead a Successful Life

Lesson: Parents cannot live their children's lives, but should validate their individualities and help them see home as a safe harbor. Worrying only makes the children feel they are under fire from all sides.

Juvenile detention center counselor Mr. Wen's lament:

The child lost his mother when he was young, and his father worked very hard to raise him. However, not knowing how to instill self-discipline in him, the well-to-do father just gave him lots of money to spend. With all that money, the kid began making problems and going astray, spending money however he pleased. The only way the father knew how to deal with the child was to give him more money.

The child began his prison life at a young age; as time went on, he had totally adjusted to this lifestyle. Inside the prison, there was discipline and order, which regrettably he could not maintain when he was released. He did not have the self-discipline.

When he was released from prison, not being his relative or friend, I had scant control over him. Our exchanges were cordial. I could only watch over him from a distance, and tried not to be too intrusive. Later on, we lost contact with each other. I tried calling him a couple of times, but he did not reply. When I saw him again, he was back in prison, serving a 27-year sentence.

I was deeply disturbed upon seeing him like that as he was essentially going to spend most of his life in prison. He was quite an exemplary inmate the last time he was in, a bright kid who knew how to help with lots of things. His supervisor had nothing but good things to say about him. It was a shame that someone as bright as he was should languish in prison again and again, a total waste of his gifts and a loss to society and the nation.

I found a chance to ask him, "Why did you come to me only when you got into trouble? Were you hoping I could somehow rein you in and tell you what you were doing was wrong? Yes? But, why couldn't you learn to have better self-control?" He was so used to indulging his wants that he could hardly see his own problems.

Parents are partly to blame, but the learning milieu at school and society at large begs for improvement. The fact is we are expecting schools to shoulder too much responsibility for teaching our kids. I often say one of the most notorious problems in Taiwan is too much talk. The parents have a lot to say to schools and to society, but when it comes to stopping before the traffic signs, how often do they cross the "forbidden line" without giving it a thought? Ego conveniently puts ourselves first. One glaring example is what one father said to his child accused of stealing, "If you want stationery, I could have just brought some back from the office for free. Why did you even need to steal?" This father had forgot the ancient wisdom of teaching by example, not words.

Social learning is one of the established theories in criminology. People develop the motivation to commit a crime through the people they associate with. When a guest visits our house, if my child just sits there, I will correct him, "Why didn't you stand up and greet our guest? He is also older than you." My kid would counter that we should all behave like friends and mingle. I was beside myself. I am older than you, and so are your aunties and uncles. How could we all be just friends? You need to get on your feet and give us the proper greetings. He would protest, saying that the decorum was excessive and that we were not in a prison. However, these are basic manners.

"You stand up and greet when you see an elder. I will be upset if you don't do that next time." Because the people around him think like that, he thinks that is normal, but that is wrong behavior and needs to be corrected! Parents need to find an effective way to get their children interested in society and establish social bond with others. The psychologist Alfred Adler stated, "Individual psychology is in fact social psychology."

How a child will turn out is not entirely all the parent's doing, but their influence is nevertheless substantial. It is true that parents could change certain behaviors, but they should not do that purely for the child's sake. They need to further understand that their changed behavior will not necessarily affect their child; it may or may not happen. There is no direct causal relationship between the change in a parent's behavior and that in the child's. It can only be possible if the parent works hard at changing but has no expectations. The child will come to the decision on their own as to whether or not they want to change.

I grew up in a very strict family. When it came time to make any decisions, my mother would always remind us to look far enough ahead and to make sure we stayed on the right path.

Please keep your sense of humor when reading the following. Smile. Everyone messes up sometimes.

If your son is clueless and immature, please join a group for discussions on how to help him. But it is just possible that you might find your own father in the same group, too.

Heart Lamp #5

Self-transcendence is the Goal of Human Existence

Lesson: No matter how difficult the situation has become, one needs to look beyond the cloudy sky and find a silver lining. Aspire to be of service to mankind, and the heart will never be constricted. Only through pious repentance will one be free from selfish ego.

Prison Counselor Mr. Chen on the preciousness of life:

One of the prisoners who brought me great distress was imprisoned for sexual assault. Right after the assault, he tried committing suicide at home by burning coal indoors, but it did not work. After his confinement, we paid special attention to his case. I accompanied him to fourteen of his doctor's visits, including seven out of the prison. I felt he was making progress, but in the end he still gave up on himself. He did not tell anyone what was tormenting him, and somehow passed all the tests as sane. Then one day, unexpectedly, he succeeded in ending his own life. It was so tragic! I blamed myself for not being able to save him despite all my efforts to help him rehabilitate.

The saddest part was his failure to find closure with his children. I think he could have left them with something positive. Even though it was impossible to change the bitter past, he could at least have told them how he was going to go on with his life. However, not one word of remorse was uttered! None. Not only did he not apologize but he chose to end his suffering by ending his own life, thinking it would be the ultimate solution. Little did he realize the far-reaching consequences of his action. His children would not learn how to cope with failures or transcend problems. This habitual tendency will affect his children's children and may predispose them to repeat the same mistakes.

I felt quite guilty and blamed myself for letting his family down even though they still thanked me because they knew how much I had tried. One life is lost, however. I still felt there must have been something more I could have done. Maybe I could have spent more time or engaged in deeper dialogues with him, so that he could have gotten a chance to make it right with his children. His family is now without a father figure and has lost half of the parent-child relationship. I fear for the long-lasting harm his action will bring.

Whatever happened will forever etch its marks in time. If one is able to see life in a new light and change one's way of thinking, one will be able to free oneself from pain. He will also be able to transform the people around him as they will learn how to face and adapt to adversities instead of quitting.

Please keep your sense of humor when reading the following. Smile. Everyone messes up sometimes.

After a man had scored a zero on a test, he sobbed bitterly, "Heaven o heavens, what have I done to deserve this?" Out came the reply, "You gave wrong answers to all the questions."

A Mission of Kindness Nurtures Kind Karma

Lesson: Everyone needs to learn to live in harmony with others in order to overcome low self-esteem and a scarcity mentality; however, only when one is not watched, yet still insists on doing the right things will that person truly be his own master. This is the quintessential quality of a life lived without regrets.

Comments from Mr. Zhou, Department of Correction officer:

To be quite honest, there are three things a government employee needs to keep in mind in order to ensure a safe tenure until retirement. Firstly, avoid illegal business practices; secondly, avoid risky dealings; thirdly, avoid doing anything that keeps one up at night. In other words, do not take on tasks that are beyond one's own authority. One must follow these three rules lest he risk his future. Do not break the law knowingly, and do not disregard safety issues knowingly. Sometimes one may forgo these considerations because the cause seems right, but it must still be lawful for the cause to have legitimacy.

In the past, a father would want his children to work for the government for its ironclad job security. This is the reason why all the kids in my family, save one, are civil servants. The maverick actually makes the most money, but I feel I am the happiest because my job gives me so many opportunities to help people. Education does not necessarily lead to ability, or experience to wisdom, or money to a stress-free life, and crime has nothing to do with ability or money either. In my lifetime of experience, I have done charity work and have been on a mission, rehabilitating people from bad to good, which makes my life worth living.

Although each inmate has a unique story, each one would affect at least three families: that of their own, their spouse's parents, and their own parents. Whenever I see them slacking off, I would admonish them, "Don't you know how crucial your role is? How can you waste time and not change? This is how you can repay the debt you owe to your parents, your family, your victim's family, your community and everything else that makes your existence possible."

Our job, in essence, is to help inmates in any capacity we can in addition to enforcing the law. In a sense, we also have a responsibility to their families. If all we do is dish out punishment, then the only thing we will have achieved is keeping them even further from their families.

I have long suspected that people are becoming more wicked. It will take a lot of effort to correct their behavior once they are in prison. It is much easier to keep them on the right path if we can get to them before they reach middle school age. Once they have strayed from the path, it is much more difficult to bring them back. We should spend more time with them and more of our resources on education, a much better approach than trying to rehabilitate them after they have gone astray. It is just much harder. I am hoping our government will really focus on this area for preventative measures, such as reworking our textbooks or setting up facilities where kids can burn off their excess energies. How they will eventually turn out has everything to do with their family and school environment.

I often tell inmates, "When it's all quiet at night, think about the people you miss; think about how you ended up here. Think about the changes you want to make. After that, if you still feel like it, jot your thoughts down. Remind yourself of the most unhappy days of your life, and swear never to go back on that same slippery slope again."

I also remind them in meditation sessions, "Actually, you are able to control your emotions. Life is hard here in prison. Think seriously about why you are wasting away your future here. Where did you go wrong? You have to be able to meditate and do some serious introspection; especially in the dead of the night, think about your parents and your family and all the people you care about. How did I end up here? What kind of mistakes did I make in the past? I hope you really think about it, and then tell yourself that you will never return to this place again."

As a counselor, I feel that I have reaped my greatest reward when I see the inmates change for the better, never to come back in here again.

Please keep your sense of humor when reading the following. Smile. Everyone messes up sometimes.

There was a little kid who aspired to grow up into a con man. He would make a lot of money and give it to the poor. The teacher commended him, saying, watch out, many of your classmates tell me they want to be cops when they grow up.

Heart Lamp #7

Feeling the Love of Others

Lesson: Believe that each person is born with innate goodness and that there is love in people's hearts. Even a devil has love in his heart and wants to express it; it is just that his way of expressing it is not commonly acceptable to most people.

From a prison counselor Mr. Lai:

There are those inmates who not only help clean the prison but also take care of the very sick by tube feeding them, bathing them, helping them go to the bathroom, or even gently encouraging them to do physical therapy. I doubt that these helpers would do those things with such care and patience even for their own family members. I am very moved. I am sure they are on their way back to rediscovering optimism and hope in life for themselves and people around them.

When they go beyond their self-centeredness and take

an interest in actually helping others, they are sure to begin solving some of their own problems in life. They see they are not the only ones being locked up, and in the process of helping others, they themselves become inspired, as do all those around them who also feel the warmth of their loving kindness. Such behavior is tremendously inspiring and heart-warming. When we meet people, we are never sure how long they will stay in our lives; through the act of helping, we are sure to leave an indelible impression in their hearts.

The inmates are not entirely to blame for their crimes. Some of them had no choice with their line of work, not realizing what they do actually hurt other people. This is the reason we need to give them the right guidance. Most of them have very low self-esteem; they often choose to give up on themselves when life's pressures became too much to bear.

When we get to know inmates better, the lines between good and evil become even more blurry. These inmates have such incredibly good work ethics; they are even more detail-oriented and motivated than people in the regular workforce. One cannot help wondering how these good people ever wound up on the wrong side of the law? As people often say, there is only a fine line between flip-flops and dress shoes. Some people crossed the line but did not get caught; others did not even step on the line but were accused and wrongly put away on suspicion alone. As the Western saying goes, "You are innocent until proven guilty."

To a medical professional, all people, including prisoners, should have the same rights to medical care. A prisoner is more than just a label. Love embraces all as equals, and it transcends religious differences and the concepts of good and bad.

Of course, initially, doctors and nurses may be apprehensive about treating prisoners. They may be afraid of possibly being kidnapped by their patients. Furthermore, if the prisoners believe that they have been treated with disrespect, the doctors or nurses fear that the prisoners may take revenge after they are released. The fact of the matter is, if we get to know the prisoners better and understand the reason behind their behavior, we would be more sympathetic. Some people just have a quick temper; some have habits that are hard to change. Many come from poor, single-parent, or skipped-generational families, and are deprived of love growing up, leading to feelings of resentment and hatred. This may be a symptom of a larger societal problems. Inmates are not necessarily completely to blame.

Here, we are witnessing the deepest secret of the human heart: that humanity is a mixture of good and evil. The dividing line between them depends on the situation, the time, the people, and varies from day to day. What does not change, however, is the indefatigable love at the bottom of our hearts.

The Creator is looking down upon us, and He does not want to be disappointed. When we believe there is love in the world, we will feel love in return. Everyone is entitled to the same medical attention. If we love selflessly without asking for anything in return, we will receive much more love back than the love that we give out. Loving others brings more love back to us than what we have given.

Please keep your sense of humor when reading the following. Smile. Everyone messes up sometimes.

When you see everyone around you as trash, you are a trash can. When you see all the people around you as enemies, you are already surrounded by enemies. When you see everyone around you as jewels, you are a treasure box. When you see everyone around you as a Bodhisattva, you are the Buddha. What you are depends on your perceptions.

Heart Lamp #8

A Goal with Purpose Will Increase One's Willpower

Lesson: The world is filled with hope. Be optimistic and positive. Finding the meaning and purpose of life brings strength to our resolve and turns on the bright light of life again.

Prison counselor Mr. Lin on joy:

There was an inmate who grew up like an orphan because both his parents were jailed on drug offenses. He had been in and out of prison from his teens into his thirties. I had always encouraged him to read motivational books because only from having ample positive energy can good things come. I saw the progress he had been making, and something wonderful did happen.

On the day of his parole release, he shared with me the good news, "My girlfriend is pregnant, and we are going to be married. Even though I am over forty and don't have much time left, I will treasure having a family because I never had a home of my own. I will not let the baby grow up as an orphan like me." He seemed to have woken up from a dream, his eyes sparkling, and face filled with joy.

Exhibiting good behavior and learning the trade of noodle-making while in prison ensured him a job after he was released. He will have a wife and be a father soon. The saying is true that a son makes everything right. He will need to take care of his new home, and this responsibility will give him the emotional tenacity he needs to begin a new life. I was so overjoyed to hear his story, as if I had won an award, and he actually never returned to prison again. He would call me from time to time to exchange greetings.

We all have our idea of the meaning of life, and we all need to find it on our own. When a person clearly sees his purpose and duty in life, despite all the hardship and humiliations he may face, his resolve will only get stronger.

Family support is very important. Some prisons hold

several family reunions a year, albeit quite short. The inmates are required to learn cultural and artistic activities before their regular classes, and their family members sit in the front rows and watch. The applause is extremely encouraging, as inmates see that their families know they are making progress, and feel the support from them. The purpose of family reunion is to let the inmates know they are not forgotten, and is a way to increase their willpower and self-discipline.

To us, the most encouraging pithy saying is, "When you save one person, you save the whole family." What we are actually doing is giving the family a chance for rebirth.

Dharma Master Cheng Yen once was asked how to have willpower. She replied, "Ask yourself first, why don't you have willpower?" It is ultimately up to each of us to conquer our inferiority complex and low self-esteem. It is of no use to hide in a daydream and pretend to be superior.

Please keep your sense of humor when reading the following. Smile. Everyone messes up sometimes.

Who would have thought a chance meeting would turn into an auspicious beginning of a lifetime where our innate nature meets and our souls connect; this is fortune smiling at us.

Heart Lamp #9

Courage To Choose A Good Path

Lesson: There are times when we make wrong decisions in life without knowing it. What we think is worth pursuing later turns out to be a liability. We have no choice but to change our pessimistic thinking and decide to take on a brand-new life and path. There are no obstacles that cannot be overcome, just unaware people who are unwilling to change.

Prison counselor Mr. Liu on self-confidence:

There was a young female inmate who refused to see her parents and only wished to see her boyfriend. Her parents split up when she was small, and. She lived with her grandmother who passed away when she was fifteen, then having to live on social welfare. At age 17, she met her boyfriend who introduced her to love and drugs. She became a user and a dealer, and was put in jail at age 21. To her, drugs and boyfriends were symbols of love, but because her boyfriend was often in and out of prison for drug offenses, he was absent from her life much of the time. She was quite lonely and sad; her depression also led her to inflict injuries upon herself.

She complained, "I know I am supposed to take the good road, but where is my good road? Why would I willingly take the hard road? Would you? Am I stupid? Why would I choose the bad road? Please tell me, where is my good road?"

I tried to comfort her, "Since you are already here, now is a good time to change your fate. No one can shoulder your sadness for you. You must learn to be mature and rely on yourself to be strong. We all must be responsible for the choices we make."

Later on, I took her to the prison bakery where she learned useful skills, sharped her mind, and was able to garner enough courage to overcome her low self-esteem. Over time, she became all the more confident.

There was also a boy whose childhood was unbearably

poignant. He really hated his family and totally shut out the world. After his mother left, he went to look for her, but when she saw him, she told him to not bother her again because she already had a new family. If her mother-in-law were to see him, it would harm her marriage. The boy was totally rejected and abandoned. When his family came to see him, of course, he did not want to see them.

His reason was: "You only care about me when I am locked up. Do you feel guilty now? Is this why you are here?" This feeling indeed explained his behavior. He has never experienced the kind of family love kids his age enjoy. He lacks a sense of community, understanding and confidence. For him, there is only self-loathing from early childhood.

There was another child who was quite talented at drawing. He joined gangs when he was ten and got tattoos all over his body. After he was charged with involuntary manslaughter, his mother committed suicide. She chose the lunar New Year's Eve to kill herself. When this happened, his father was still out in a gang. He called me, grief-stricken. I quickly rushed over to his place.

He told me, "You are my only family. I've made more than twenty calls, but not even my own family showed up. You are the only one." That really broke my heart. I hugged him and encouraged him to turn his despair into hope. Be courageous and strong, I told him. Make use of your talent in drawing. Be brave, and embrace the future with purpose.

Life contains infinite possibilities, but it is only with the spirit of altruism that we can walk the good road and rewrite our stories.

Please keep your sense of humor when reading the following. Smile. Everyone messes up sometimes.

This is the advertisement of a vendor selling umbrellas, "Sunny days, 20% off. Rainy days, 10% off. Gloomy days, use the sunscreen and save money to buy an umbrella.

Heroes Can Face the Difficulty of Conquering Inner Demons

Lesson: All heroes eventually meet their nemesis, which is their inner demon. A true measure of their strength is self-discipline. So long as they are not able to rein in their desires, they will forever remain a slave. By exerting control over ourselves, we can be in the driver's seat, and then we are the true heroes who have endless possibilities..

Mr. Lin the psychologist on how we are our greatest enemy:

According to the Ministry of Justice, there are currently 27,633 people incarcerated in prisons for drug offenses. The ease with which we can get our hand on drugs is a cause. At first, the price seems quite reasonable, but that is because the dealers want to get people hooked. After the addiction takes hold, they immediately raise the price, and users have no choice but to keep buying. This problem really begs for a solution, but there is none. If there were an easy solution, none of the countries in the world would need to budget for or engage in political discussions on drug enforcement.

There once was a male drug addict who boasted of being a macho guy who could beat up anyone, and even the police were afraid of him. But now, he's been defeated by the power of addiction.

He insisted, "It's not me. The drugs are just too beautiful. I can't control myself. I don't know how to say no or change. I am beaten. Why did they have to invent drugs to get me in prison?" I retorted, "Are you saying that you'll let your addiction get the better of you? Are you going to just live in prison? You have to pay a price later for something you can't say 'no' to now." He was speechless. I continued, "Don't let your cravings possess you, and don't forfeit your future. Be accountable. Here, you need to learn to think less about yourself. When you are the boss of yourself, no one can defeat you. The moment you let your heart run wild, you will be controlled by your inner demon of emotions and desires, and you'll lose your freedom."

Actually, those who have weak self-control often have more self-determination than the strong ones. But they do not have a definite purpose in life, and they want others to take responsibility for their life. They do not want any obligations, yet are ready to enjoy the fruits of the labor of society.

Another male drug addict thought it was unreasonable that he was put in jail, "I didn't kill anyone or burn anything down. I didn't do anything bad except drugs. What I do with my body is my business. Why am I here?"

"The drugs you are using are really powerful stuff. Not only will they destroy your body and organs, you will also lose your mind and end up hurting other people, and be a menace to society. By saying you don't want to quit, are you saying you don't want to live?" There is a Jewish saying, "If I am not for myself, who will be for me?" When you lose your humanity, you lose your sense of right and wrong. All you care about is what you want, and you will hurt people. But we are here to protect people." I addressed his question with this unequivocal answer.

Neurotic people often claim that so long as their intention is good, they can say whatever they want with impunity. However, we all know that when someone does things based only on the language and reasoning he understands, most likely he is either a psychopath or a criminal. They have no empathy for other people and have a total disregard for rules or social norms. Their bodies and minds are dysfunctional, and all they want is avoidance. We have a responsibility to get them to take a vested interest in society. We furthermore want to train their mind to be sharp. In the Buddhist sutra, it says, "If you wish to understand all the Buddhas of the three times, know that everything arises from the mind alone." In the Bible, it also cautions, "Above all else, guard your heart, for everything you do flows from it." Albert Einstein purportedly said, "The definition of insanity is doing the same thing over and over again and expecting a different result."

Please keep your sense of humor when reading the following. Smile. Everyone messes up sometimes.

He claims he has 100 million yuan in the bank. The most important use of that money is to heal his delusional disorder.

Filial Love Cannot Wait

Lesson: Parents work hard and diligently to give their children better lives. Children need to be grateful and repay the debt of gratitude.

Correction officer Mr. Lin on how children with filial gratitude accumulate merit:

A-hon's mother is well over eighty years old, and had little education. She gives him 3,000 yuan (New Taiwan Dollar) each month when she comes to see him; the transportation alone costs her at least another 1,000 yuan. Despite all that, he still keeps asking for more things and more money. It is obvious he is a spoiled brat who thinks only about himself.

He even complained, "Even if I were at home, I wouldn't know what to say to her. Tell her to just bring me the money when she comes. She always gets me food and stuff. What the heck. That really pisses me off. I am giving all her things to other inmates. With a mother like that, there is no getting through to her."

I quickly counseled him, "This is because she did not go to school. That is how it was in her times. Her job was to raise kids, making sure there is food on the table and shoes on your feet. Now you are turning around and blaming her. That shows you are not too well educated yourself. Because you have had an education, you shouldn't feel she is doing anything wrong. With our educated mind, we should be able to see that she is right. She never went to school, and we should be the ones teaching her. What's more, she gave her all in raising you, and now she is old. It's bad enough you are not paying back her kindness, but you are still letting her worry about you, coming all this way just to see you. Think about it. How much longer do you want her to worry about you? How much longer will you still get to do nice things for her? Don't wait until she is gone to feel sad. This kind of unfulfilled love will make you regret it for the rest of your life." He was silent for a long time.

"The only way to show her your love is to repent your

mistakes. Truly change and be a new person. This is the only thing you can do now to repay her kindness. Don't wait until it's too late."

At the next family reunion, unexpectedly, he actually hugged her mother and told her how much he appreciated her. Seeing that, my eyes welled up with tears.

My job really allows me to witness the agonies many families go through. I see them waiting outside, and really feel for them. The visit lasts only thirty minutes, but I see aging parents traveling from far away carrying food baskets queuing to see their kids who may not even want to see them. Of course, that largely depends on how they were brought up and the relationship they had with their parents.

I have also seen another inmate, A-ren, who would throw the food into the trash can when he got back to his dorm. I brought him over and asked him why. He told me what he wanted was money. What good was the food?

I counseled him, "You are a man. When your parents gave birth to you, they must have been very happy, because there was one more son to help out with the family. Has it ever occurred to you that not only have you not helped, but you've made them spend money on you? There is no gain but only loss for them. Have you thought about that? There is an old saying that is not very flattering to kids, "It is better to have a daughter than a son. A daughter will at least take care of the family, but a son will not, and can even make trouble." Is that so? I often use this adage as a motivational tool for male inmates.

"What else are you expecting your parents to do for you? Your father works really hard! The money doesn't come easily, and he has to take care of your children, and also has to give you the 3,000 yuan monthly allowance. Have you ever thought what he had to go through to earn that money?"

Soon after, A-ren's mother passed away. I stayed with him, and we talked about life and his mother. Thinking of her made him emotionally quite agitated. I remember vividly. It was six o'clock in the morning. I took him to the Kaohsiung City Mortuary, and when they wheeled his mother out, he kneeled down and banged his forehead on the ground repeatedly, as if to express his remorse. I pulled him up, "Right now, you can't do anything for your mother. Perhaps you want to chant the name of the Buddha in her memory. You also need to make up your mind to change. This is how you can comfort her soul in heaven." I stayed with him for another hour and a half, and also got him some candies and crackers as an offering to his mother.

Later on, whenever other inmates complained about the harshness of the correctional punishment, A-ren would take my side, "Our captain is actually a really nice guy. He may look mean, but he's got a kind heart. He's helped me a lot." Perhaps it was due to his effort we were able to avert unrest at the disciplinary quarters. Out of the few thousand inmates, so long as I am able to bring about change in one or two of them, all my effort will have been worthwhile.

This year, I feel that heaven above has been really kind to me. After my bout with acute hepatitis, I was out of the hospital in just fourteen days. A female volunteer came to my house and told my mother that I truly had a lot of merit as it had only taken me two weeks to heal. That made me feel that I have been on the right path and should put out more effort whenever I can. Even though I work in law enforcement, and will not always see eye to eye with the inmates, I will do what I need to do to reform them. Of course, there have been some pushbacks and negative feedback from the inmates, but time will prove everything. Love is my communication tool. I tell my mother that we will be OK so long as we think good thoughts.

I was raised by my maternal grandmother, and my elder brother by his paternal grandmother. We both did fine without the usual issues confronting skipped-generational families because we were grateful. So long as we keep gratitude in mind and try to repay the kindness, Heaven will not shortchange us.

I have seen so many people going through here, and have often engaged in introspection. Am I attentive to my family? Am I doing enough for them? Am I doing all that I can at my job?

Please keep your sense of humor when reading the following. Smile. Everyone messes up sometimes.

It is of great importance where you wait for your opportunity. Waiting at the wrong place means never arriving. It is like waiting for the subway at a bus station, or a ship at the airport. Someone might poke fun at you and ask if you are waiting for a blimp?

Corruption and Crime Are Learned Behavior

Lesson: Read more books. There is an old saying, "Read a book a hundred times, and it shall reveal itself to you." The more we read, the more renewed confidence we get from it. We are often too easily swayed by what other people say. The goal of a lifetime of learning is to conquer this fear and anxiety.

Supervisor Mr. Li Zheng Feng on how education remedies bad judgments:

I feel that corruption and crime are learned behaviors, which in turn are the result of our habitual tendencies. At my job, I am confined in the same space as the inmates. Handling them really takes some skill. Since the staff hold all the cards, they need to show kindness and be ready to help, and the inmates will respond in kind. I believe this iron rule will also work in any workplace, with any employee.

Civil servants all have different personalities. There are those who will give you a hand just before you are about to fall, and then there are those who will wait until after you've fallen to pull you up. It is difficult to judge who is right or wrong. If someone wants recognition, then they will just wait until things get terribly wrong. Until then, they will sit around and do nothing. They will act only when something goes wrong. There are many government employees who behave like that, but I believe in doing my job right. If someone were to cross the line, I, for sure, would send them to the prosecutor's office or the Agency Against Corruption office. If the court finds them not guilty, then it is their luck, and not my business anymore. But when I know someone has crossed the line, I will have no choice but to enforce the law because this is a duty conferred on me by the state.

The directors and supervisors here are all white-collar, but after having spent time with inmates from different walks of life, we are beginning to change our thinking. As we change our families will be affected, too. This is the reason we need to constantly engage in self-reflection;

we have to respect the seriousness and sanctity of our job. Heaven is looking down upon what we do, and will not want to be disappointed. This is how it is. We need to set a boundary between good and evil for the inmates to abide by, and furthermore help them become productive members of society. This is the purpose of our job. We need to constantly remind ourselves of the importance of our job, but we cannot go beyond the boundary for civil servants, and that can be difficult sometimes. The more interactions we have with them, the more fluid that boundary becomes. There are times when the lives of the inmates and ours become indistinguishable. There is a distinct difference between what we do during the day and after work. This is most challenging. In the course of helping them, we are sometimes mired in our convoluted and subtle feelings of sympathy for them. We need to learn to control our emotions appropriately so as not to tempt them into taking advantage of our kindness. We have to constantly remind ourselves of the importance of adhering to rules. There is much for us to consider and learn.

This is the reason everyone needs to get motivated to learn, to get more educated. An example would be these hoodlums who have great energy. The key is education. With the right education, they can be like Robin Hood, if we appeal to their sense of pride. Of course, the process of motivating them can be quite trying. Not everyone survives the training of the special forces. In Taiwan, quite a few kids are hooked into computer games of combat with impressive sensory effects and scores of killings. What the game taught them is to kill all the enemies without mercy; however, life is not a game where one needs to wipe out all their enemies. There will be friends and foes, and sometimes a friend can turn into an enemy. Interpersonal relationship is really the most pressing subject we need to study.

So long as we are human, we will use our emotions to validate our attitudes. Since I have witnessed so much here, I am less demanding of my children, but I taught them about having the proper values at a young age. I respect the universal order of heaven, earth, troops, parents and teachers, and do not ever allow my children to address me by my name; it has to be "father." I will correct them if they do not. We are Chinese after all, and must observe basic decorum; it is the last defense of our culture, and should be the aim of today's school system. This is because the law only addresses superficial issues, not the core.

Many parents put too much pressure on their kids; they either give up or push back, or even escape from their parents and end up on the wrong path. This is the reason we need to give children a second chance when they make a mistake; everyone makes mistakes. Of course, we will talk about what they did wrong. So long as they do not keep repeating them or engaging in anything illegal, I am not like other parents with excessive demands. The kids may be naughty, but all I ask is that they be good people; their grades are secondary. Good morals come first; then we can ask for better grades. Naturally we want to encourage them to study, but we cannot force them because character is the most important. They should not bully the weaker ones. When the kids are ill and lying in their beds, we do not ask anything but for them to get better. When their health returns, we can then ask them to study and do good deeds. When one tries to the best of one's ability, there will be unexpected rewards. That is life.

The more books I read, the more benefit I get. Although religion is touted as a confidence builder, personally, without hardship I would not have prayed to the Buddha. After having read the book, "Orthodox Chinese Buddhism," I have changed. I have become gentler. When I was a kid, I was great in martial arts, but I never hit anyone. One time, however, I was beat up very badly by a group of accused criminals who almost killed me. I know that not fighting back was the right thing to do, and Heaven has been kind to me; it gives me a stronger body, and my arms and legs feel even more powerful. The military officer would say, "A soldier should not kill indiscriminately for fear of bad karma. A soldier should not be killed lightly for fear of his honor."

One can still learn to be gentle when facing a challenge. Dharma Master Cheng Yen says, "Only by forgiving others can we be kind to ourselves." When we are ill, we get to experience the pain of sickness. Wisdom comes from experience. That is so true. I have already learned to make people laugh. I feel the ability to bring laughter to people is a blessing.

Please keep your sense of humor when reading the following. Smile. Everyone messes up sometimes.

The tragedy of life is not being able to do anything when a problem keeps presenting itself. An even bigger tragedy is not being able to act on situations despite possessing all the skills in the world. The biggest tragedy, however, is hurting people you do not mean to hurt when you finally decided to act.

Heart Lamp #13

Do Not Rub Salt Into Your Own Wounds

Lesson: We should not despair of the loss of our physical freedom, but rather cherish our spiritual assets, turn our negative thoughts into a positive mindset, and ponder upon human nature from an altruistic perspective.

Social worker Mr. Lin on encouragement over humiliation:

It was this 17-year-old inmate's third time in, a kid in juvenile detention. He cried uncontrollably when first brought in at age 14 for a drug offense, but at age sixteen he was in again, also on a drug charge. By age seventeen, it was his third. He had always struggled with drugs, and later on became a dealer. Because he had no money, he joined a gang. It actually did not matter what his family was like; all the details were in his verdict document. We really should not keep asking him, "What was your crime? What did you do to get in here?" To him it was like a wound, a label that could never be rubbed off. He had been through what only an adult should have, going from the police station to the prosecutor's office, from the court to the sentencing desk to the executor's office, and then to the detention center, always being asked again and again about his crime. Why? People keep on wanting to ask him the same questions, which causes more trauma with an unbearable heaviness, as if rubbing salt into his wound, reintroducing the pain by making him relive his crime. Some people feel they have already faced up to their crime once; by the second, third and fourth time, they are already feeling quite lowly and insecure. They do not trust people anymore; they give up on themselves, thinking they might as well be as wicked as they can be. They figure they will be back in prison in no time after they are released.

We find an analogy here with handling fights among kids. I don't begin by asking them why they fight. I first address their emotions. What happened to you guys today? Once they have calmed down, they will tell me on their own. One kid told me the reason he joined a gang was that other people were throwing rocks at his house.

The fact is they all have debilitating inferiority complexes, and, as a result, are reactive, arrogant and aggressive. We find they all try to be bigger than they really are. The aggressive ones will attack people unexpectedly to show who is in control. Their lack of patience comes from their low self-esteem; they feel that they are not strong or good enough, and they try very hard to defeat those feelings. Attacking people is the easiest way for them to assert their worth, respectability and superiority. We need to, however, think of the right approach to help them heal because they cannot yet see that all people are one integral whole, and that there is a natural order to everything. We cannot castigate or invalidate them, for they will be even more defensive in order to hide their inferiority. We can only be kind and gentle with our point of view, and try to let them see their hang-ups. We also encourage them to try to help people.

One ponders who might be the most powerful people in a civilized society, the answer could be babies. The reason is because babies are not controlled by others. They are the real bosses of themselves.

The fact is, everyone is insecure about something, but the feeling of insecurity is not a disease; rather, it can beneficially motivate people to achieve greater upward mobility. So long as all their efforts are unselfish and are in service of mankind, their value system will not deviate from what is good for the society. Crimes are a result of distorted values.

Please keep your sense of humor when reading the following. Smile. Everyone messes up sometimes.

Some things happen to us and we don't know whether to laugh or cry such as getting a weight off your chest, but it rolls off and hits your foot, giving you a heartache.

Heart Lamp #14

Those Who Only Care About Themselves Will Not Survive In Society

Lesson: We belong to this world we live in, and we are not the center of the universe. Those who are self-centered will not be able to fit in and become productive members of society.

Prison counselor Mr. Wu on a problem without an easy answer:

Yu-hong had always been a naughty child. His father, being from the northeastern part of China known for strong-tempered people, would often tie and hang him up and beat him until he was half dead. His parents were not divorced; both are quite old now. Due to his inability to be around others, Yu-hong had lived alone for most of his 20+ years behind bars. He would fight with others and refused to do much work.

Yu-hong was divorced, with a son, and according to him, had done well in the past. As he came up for parole, he needed to have a different permanent address outside of the prison (the default address for long-term prisoners is the prison, as required by law in the 1980-1990s). However, his father, who had been utterly disappointed in him, refused to let his son use his address and hukou (residential record) because of the son's habit of making lawsuits. For instance, the son had wanted a few thousand dollars (New Taiwan Dollars) from his father, and, when refused, he sued his father for unlawfully keeping his money.

This inmate talked about once owning a car and now wanting it back. He also accused his wife of stealing money from his post office savings account, and wanted to sue her, too. This was a case of personality disorder. His only concern was about himself and his own gains. He could not be reasoned with and could not be disciplined.

I have been counseling him since 2014, and we got along reasonably well. I supplied him with some stationery and phone cards because no one would give him money. I also got him batteries for his radio because he had no money. However, about half a year ago, when he was about to sign the counseling memo after a particularly lengthy session, he saw that I left out an earlier part of our conversation. He then decided to totally forget all the nice things I had done for him, and accused me of harassing him in prison. In the end, he filed frivolous lawsuits against all of us.

Normally, prisoners are very grateful to their counselors. Prisoners nowadays are armed with human rights protections and would sue any prison personnel at the slightest provocation. In the past, prisons were relatively closed off, and if things had to be done, so long as it was the right thing, we would just do it. Now, there are monitors everywhere and everything we do must strictly adhere to rules and regulations for fear of getting sued.

He still does not have an outside permanent address. When I contacted his father, he unequivocally told me that no one in his family welcomes him. When I called his son, he was incredulous, "Do you think my father has changed?

Is he really to be paroled?" The inmate's son has a newborn baby, and does not want his father to disrupt his family. When we asked the inmate's father to provide hukou consent for him to move in, he wrote, "Consent Not Given," and noted that whoever released him should be responsible for his son. Now that his family is not an option, I arranged for him to have an interview with a pastor, who was himself once an inmate. He agreed to help, but three days later, after having looked him up online, he had a change of heart. There is no one this inmate could turn to for an outside address. Without one, he cannot be eligible for parole, for there is no way to track him. According to one parole provision, the parolee must have a permanent address and a regular job. He must report to the parole officer in the city where he intends to reside, for example, Yilan prosecutor's office, if he were to live in Yilan, at first once every two weeks, and then regularly once a month or every three months, and so on. A permanent address is mandatory.

Generally, it will not be easy for inmates to find regular jobs. Even if there were ten or twenty job opportunities inmates would need to forget their own social stigma as a basic confidence builder. Their bosses would want to know their past, but once they were accepted as employees, their past should never be a future hang-up between them and their boss. It is unlikely that the inmate could find a job where there is no boss, nor one where teamwork was not required. Owing to this self-centered personality, inmates would not be able to forge a good relationship with people. They would not be reliable co-workers because they always place their own interests above those of the company. They usually do not belong on the winning team.

Please keep your sense of humor when reading the following. Smile. Everyone messes up sometimes.

There are those who are at fault but insistently deny any wrongdoings and claim to be the victims. Those people shall forever remain victims.

Heart Lamp #15

Marks of Impression—Tattoos

Lesson: Each challenge marks the beginning of healing as well as growth. What is important is to reclaim sovereignty over our selves. In the face of others' expectations, what can we do to remain true to ourselves without losing it in the future?

Juvenile detention center counselor Mr. Zhong's recounts:

It is not easy to accept a rehabilitated prisoner. It is akin to seeing a person with severely burned facial scars. We should not act patronizingly, and yet at the same time we need courage to meet that facially disfigured person. The nature of a counselor's job is total acceptance. It is a profession that requires tact, not only kindness. Kindness without circumspection may inadvertently inflict pain on the inmate once again. When an inmate faces an outright rejection, he is traumatized once more.

A young man who was released from the juvenile

detention center wanted me to help him look for work, I arranged for him to meet a teacher. She promised me with absolute assurance that she could find him a good job, but when I took him to her, she was terrified, saying to his face that he must get rid of his tattoos first before coming back to see her again. The young man was devastated, and stopped talking to me after that. I, too, was exceedingly discouraged and hurt.

One day, I tried to get some answers from another tattooed guy. He told me there is no way he would ever remove them!

"Teacher, I will never get rid of my tattoos. They are part of me. When I was eleven, I joined a gang, and each tattoo marks one of my many emotional ups and downs. Each mark represents parts of me growing up. They belong to my life and my life story. There is no way I can just erase all of my past memories. Teacher, I will face my life. I don't care how other people see me. I am who I am."

I was shocked by what this young fellow said about

taking responsibility for his own life. It may take him one million NT (New Taiwan) dollars to remove all his tattoos, but it is not about money or the pain of removal; he had revealed the secret of his life without fear.

We are not the ones to judge tattooed people. The fact is, truth shall reveal itself. Young people can decide to take responsibility for their actions; it is an accountability issue, but the most important thing is their attitude towards life.

Tattoos represents a statement, but social norms still associate tattoos with rebels or undesirables. Young people may get it done on a whim because some celebrities have it, but overlook the negative effect it could have on them. Recently, there are more people who regret their tattoos, yet the cost of removal can be phenomenal, although some clinics and charities are offering limited free tattoo removal services.

Tattoos in Taiwan often contain cultural symbols popular among the mafia such as a demon's head, dragon, or phoenix images, which differ from American culture. There was even one demon king figure that was touted by a religious leader as representative of the Avalokiteshvara bodhisattva. The intended effect of having a tattoo is to show one's rank within a gang. Tattoos serve as status symbols inside gangs. Those without tattoos are seen as underlings. For example, if fifty gang members go as a mob to collect a debt, those in the back (without tattoos) may get only an NT$800 cut, while those in front (with tattoos) can pull in up to NT$2,000–5,000 because of their seniority.

The reason youngsters join gangs is for a sense of belonging and recognition. They do not fit in with fellow students and do poorly at school. They probably also get scolded at home, "Why won't you study? Why do you get bad grades?" At school, while everyone else is studying for the exam, they would be the only ones doing nothing because they are too far behind to catch up. Some teachers are nice, and will let them rest their heads on their desks, but some students will object, accusing them of being the rotten apples that spoil the barrel. That will leave these students with no choice and nowhere to go and eventually join gangs!

Please keep your sense of humor when reading the following. Smile. Everyone messes up sometimes.

There is a fortune teller who can tell your fortune by looking at your face and hands. His sign reads, "We live in a society where looks matter."

Letting Go of Ego is the Volunteer Spirit

Lesson: Don't be afraid of not making progress on self-improvement. One should be more afraid of not beginning the journey. Mortal love is limited and will be exhausted. Selfless love requires cultivation of a volunteering spirit. Caring for others more than oneself transforms limited love into great love.

Supervisor Mr. Chen on volunteerism as a life commitment:

For almost twenty-eight years, I have been working in the same environment, which has allowed me the opportunity to vastly learn and grow. In the past, I accomplished most tasks assigned by my supervisors, usually ahead of schedule so they would not be disappointed. I even earned a nickname called "Mission Accomplished." However, one morning six years ago, out of the blue, I was called in to sign an agreement to be transferred to a new position. Although I was sick to my stomach when I heard the news, I tried to hide it. This new role made me feel as if all my Kung-Fu powers (metaphorically speaking) had been defused. Although I would be performing the same duties of managing inmates in a similar setting, I felt like a new born baby starting from scratch. I struggled and felt powerless in these new surroundings. Even a month into the new job I was still unable to keep up with the work demands or competently operate the computer system. It was evident that I needed to relearn everything. So, for the next three years, I befriended my colleagues, tried to get their help and encouragement, and treated them to a nice meal each year.

At first, I was quite depressed. I constantly felt powerless and afflicted with negative emotions. It wasn't until later when I tried to get involved with hosting reunion events, organizing activities, facilitating guided tours and exercising interpersonal skills that I was able to rediscover my enthusiasm for work. By reaching out, I was actually able to learn more. I was able to broaden my horizons and not just be limited to working with the inmates. What impacted me the most while participating in those events was witnessing each volunteer's gentleness. Many of them were retired teachers and pillars of society. The Tzu Chi volunteers are especially impressive in their humbleness and selflessness. I used to think I was doing very well, but actually I was arrogant and self-aggrandizing. However, when compared to the volunteers, I felt embarrassed. They were all very capable yet displayed such humility. Shouldn't those of us who got paid to work be more efficient? Volunteers give of themselves without expecting anything in return, and aspire to be of service to others. After witnessing their willingness to help in the communities and serve based on pure Bodhisattva intentions, I was inspired to want to do more. I am now grateful to learn whenever I come across new tasks at work. After having a new perspective, I am now more aware of my wrong views in the past. By understanding the importance of gratitude, I gained newfound enthusiasm. My heart is now content without the need to have anything else.

We are very familiar with the inmates owing to many years of supervising and training them. Volunteers who are unfamiliar with our system would need time to adapt. They would not know what the inmates need. Therefore, I tried my best to be of better help to the volunteers. For my self-improvement, I also attended a Teacher Student Etiquette training and obtained a tea ceremony certificate so I could teach the volunteers. Although every inmate has different habits, volunteers can educate them about etiquette, such as how to sit properly, focus in class and maintain proper decorum. As busy counselors, we want to design an etiquette system that can be taught by volunteers who can take the place of mothers, helping inmates to correct any misbehavior.

Once I encountered an inmate hyperventilating in his prison cell. It was probably due to an asthma attack, and other inmates thought he was dying. I was taught during employee training to respond to such matters immediately. Emergency actions should be performed with calmness. If the prisoner dies, I must survey the scene and keep evidence. I worked overtime that day, calmly telling other inmates not to panic and that everything would be fine once he was taken outside. I remember that they were in their cells watching me handle the situation. It was truly a tragedy to witness an inmate dying. I opened the door and started performing CPR. The person's face had a grayish tint as I was not sure if he had stopped breathing. However, I was alone and couldn't call for help. Even if someone were to look for help, the on-site nurse was on the other side of the facility. The window of opportunity to help is only a few minutes so I continued to perform CPR with mouth-to-mouth resuscitation. I repeated it again and again, thinking that even if the person were to stop breathing, I would still want to continue. Because this was my duty, I kept going until the nurse arrived, and started contacting all the people for follow-up.

Unexpectedly, that dying prisoner sat in front of me the next day. I told him, "Even with your runny nose, I still did mouth-to-mouth CPR on you. You actually came back to life. There is much to be grateful for!" I still remember receiving two commendations from my supervisor for that incident. Commendations are nothing compared to a person's life being saved, which to me, is a much more gratifying reward. Thinking back, I wasn't even afraid if this person had AIDS. The first priority was to save a person's life. Nowadays, there is no requirement that we do CPR with mouth-to-mouth rescue breathing. Directly pressing down on the center of the victim's chest is sufficient. Nevertheless, I was really nervous when the inmate looked dead. That was a very memorable situation.

Another incident involved a lady with a gangster background locked up in prison. Possibly due to her unstable emotions, she banged on the door, attacked the security cameras, splashed water and feces all over and wreaked all kinds of havoc. She claimed she was sentenced unjustly. We told her to follow the legal procedures because her conviction had been affirmed by the Supreme Court in Taiwan. One can hire a lawyer to file for an appeal and litigation, possibly presenting stronger evidence. We tried all kinds of counseling, but she wouldn't listen. Finally, we helped her write letters to the President of Taiwan, and to a tabloid magazine, "Next," as well as other places that might help her, saying that she was wrongfully convicted.

Whether wrongfully imprisoned or not, an inmate will go crazy if he or she does not accept their sentence.

This person will act out almost insanely. Usually ten out of two thousand male inmates will behave like this. The medical literature describes this kind of extreme behavior as melancholia or manic-depressive psychosis. Although we don't use the word 'lunatic', someone like this definitely behaves like one, engaging in many insane acts. He is able to do everything, short of dying, such as attacking people, kicking doors and looking for a fight with anyone. This is the kind of inmate who is depressed and consistently wanting to die. You would think he is a rule breaker but actually, he believes it is hopeless to live in this environment, dealing with his lawsuit. To address this kind of disturbing behavior, we need to first provide guidance on life management with reinforced security. Secondly, we should assign volunteers to offer psychological consultation. Thirdly, we should provide medical treatment, and lastly, arrange for him to receive the comfort of family. We provide these four kinds of services at the same time. We cannot treat this kind of inmate as a lunatic. Merely locking this person up, beefing up the security and activating suicide prevention measures are not enough. We must counsel them based on these four different considerations at once. The degree of insanity for these individuals is like that of an actual crazy lunatic. The size of prison staff and counselors is hardly enough to meet the demands of these inmates. Treating their emotions requires patience along with sufficient human resources. There are more than two thousand male inmates in every prison, but the toughest ten of them will consume most of the resources. We need the greatest patience.

After these experiences, I came across Buddhism. The Buddhist sutras have religious doctrines just like the Bible. They both have very inspiring teachings which ameliorate our anxieties. I was able to lead the inmates in chanting Buddhist mantra and transcribing the sutras. In those moments, I felt that the world was so peaceful. I believe having a religious belief helps people live together harmoniously. Those with a religious belief live life with less anxiety.

Dharma Master Cheng Yen says, "Religion is the foundation of life, and an education on how to live."

Please keep your sense of humor when reading the following. Smile. Everyone messes up sometimes.

If it makes you unhappy going to work, why are you still going to work? Because I get to feel happy after I get off work.

Heart Lamp #17

Industry Overcomes All Obstacles

Lesson: Teachings are meant to be practiced. Heaven and earth will reward those who are industrious and kind. Behavioral changes come from lifestyle changes. A change starts with putting your nose to the grindstone!

Operation manager Mr. Zhan on work:

People who work hard have no time for misconducts. Many inmates are self-centered. They pursue illusory goals, and live a life of useless values. For their life to change, I believe they must first break their outer shell. Secondly, they need to break it from the inside. How to achieve this is by working. Work can break the shell on the outside. Develop good work ethics. Breaking from the inside means rebirth and getting rid of one's ego. Train everyone to live with others harmoniously, and to be grateful to one another.

Leonardo da Vinci said, "Iron rusts from disuse, stagnant

water loses its purity, and in cold weather becomes frozen; even so does inaction sap the vigors of the mind."

The fact is, in prison, everyone has to work, as stipulated by the law. Additionally, they need to learn skills so that they can make a living when released. What they learn must be relevant and up-to-date with the current trend of society. While learning to work with everyone, they will also learn to be less self-centered.

The law specifically prohibits inmates from working under these four conditions: holidays, a death in the direct family, illness and rehabilitation.

Tzu Chi volunteers regularly come to teach inmates vegetarian cooking. Some female inmates went from not even knowing how to properly hold a cleaver to mastering the whole kitchen. Their culinary skills rival even those of restaurant chefs. One former inmate wrote that since opening his steaming buns eatery, business has been brisk, and he is able to make a living. Reading that letter was so hugely gratifying to us.

We take a pragmatic approach to teaching inmates. First, they need to learn the skills that are already familiar to society or traditional craftsmanship in danger of extinction. We stay away from the esoteric, less popular or highly technical skills. If the inmates apply themselves, something like reflexology (foot massage) can be learned easily. What is really popular today is wellness massage therapy. Not only is it a useful skill, it can also benefit their parents and family members, and in doing so also help heal their emotional rifts. We also choose traditional crafts that may soon be forgotten or woodcraft which does not go out of style. We let the inmates have the freedom to create their own designs. However, due to our limited space, we have to choose who gets to be trained. They also have to have a sentence of less than one year.

We used to say it takes three years to learn a trade, but here we have only one year. Even if they don't totally get it at first, so long as they are interested and totally focused, one year should be sufficient to learn it. Training classes are three months for each session; some last two sessions, such as the baking class. We have six instructors. If a student learns two skills from each instructor, he will have learned twelve skills, enough to make a living for himself. We try to keep them interested and motivated; they really can support themselves after getting out. Without work, their recidivism rate will be high. We certainly also want to be fair to inmates with long sentences. They work in the factory. If they are healthy, they can also assemble electronic parts, fold paper bags or make paper lotus flowers, etc. to keep them busy.

For inmates who have special skills and are serving long sentences, we have created a business for them to run. They can apply their special skills and create value. Of course we will give them special treatment, but their numbers are few. We may hire them as independent contractors to create valuable products and services.

In the vocational training facility, we find inmates who work very well with other people. Even if at first they were pretending, after some time it will become real. It could be their personality; some people are just very hard-working. Because of the possibility of parole, they also have no choice but to stay on the prison's good side. Drug dealers are more cunning, though. Due to their habits, they are used to saying different things to different people. They know whose good side they have to be on, or how to get things without having to work for them. They are habitual liars with endless stories to tell. They will keep this up for as long as possible until they have no choice but to be part of the production team. After an honest day's work, though, they will find they are ready to tell the truth.

Life is like a merry-go-round in the prison with people coming and going, staying long or short depending on their sentences, and no big, great future for them. They can only work hard, day by day as life passes by. For those of us who have a good life and good health, we should hold on to our chance all the more of fully applying our potential. This is how we can repay the gratitude of heaven for taking care of us with all nature's wonder and nourishment.

Please keep your sense of humor when reading the following. Smile. Everyone messes up sometimes.

One may claim he is not motivated or willing to do anything because he is at peace with this world. He is above the fray and will only take and never give. He is like a frog being slowly cooked in steadily heating water; he will eventually die in his own comfort.

Heart Lamp #18

Shine Your Light Wherever You Are

Lesson: True evil is the indifference of the soul, only a heart of gratitude can feel the warmth of the light.

Prison warden Mr. Xie on motivation and gratitude:

I am more focused on management. Maximizing the ultimate benefits of a prison and improving the relationships between the people and the situations are my favorite things to do. For more than a decade, no matter which prison I was transferred to, I'd have to find my own enthusiasm and creativity at every stage. I believe life has its own special meaning, and it must be sown by our own efforts. Because a prison has only so many people and a limited budget, we must find a practical way to make the best use of all resources so that the prisoners may see the light themselves and have a little more hope every day.

Education is a combination of words, examples and situational learning. It is like the pine trees that grow in a valley and the ones that grow on a hill; even though they're of the same species, different growing environments will give rise to different life forms. Evidently, situational learning will affect individual human growth.

The prison is an enclosed school. The teachers' duty is to train the prisoners, to help them stand up through hardship and difficult times. This is where situational learning is important. If we can help the prisoners live a slightly better life with a little better pay, they will feel the beauty of this world and have hope for tomorrow when they are released. The goal is to let prison workers feel more accomplished in their jobs, not satisfied with only getting a fixed monthly salary. The entire prison needs to be making progress every month.

When I first arrived at Kinmen Prison, I tried to streamline the inmates' business craft operations. Initially they were only folding ritual paper money and making origami lotuses (Asian traditions for the deceased) but later I added   stringing crystal ornaments which generated ten times the income they were making before. This greatly boosted my confidence because the inmates' families did not have to supplement their living expenses anymore. I also invited teachers to show them how to make Kinmen noodles. We later came up with carrot noodles, red bream noodles, and even spinach noodles, and they all sold well which made everybody smile with happiness. Kinmen noodles now bring in NT$10 million each year. It is incredible.

However, a teacher was puzzled, "If I show them my business, won't they compete with me after they are released?"

People in different situations will have different opinions, obviously. "Because of your skills and generosity, they have an opportunity to learn. Learning a trade is tricky. Perchance one had the talents but never got a chance. They are not competing with you. You are teaching them the skill that can help them make a living later. They know some basics, but who knows if they will really go into business; of course making money is appealing. To have this skill is very valuable to them because it enhances their confidence, and will help them re-enter society to become productive citizens. If we have fewer criminals in society will this society be more peaceful and harmonious? You are really generating boundless merit."

An inmate wrote to me, "I am very grateful. Besides paying back my restitution, I was able to send some money home this year for my children to go to school." When I left Kinmen, I received many letters thanking me for all the efforts I had put in for the inmates, but it was the dedication of the entire team and the liberty which I was given that had enabled us to accomplish a great many things. A sense of gratitude keeps the personnel doing more than just a minimum job and further supports and motivates them to keep moving forward.

Because of my knowledge in space management another prison, I was able to use a minimal budget to complete the expansion of its plant operations within eight months and increased their soy sauce production. Some inmates at that prison told me that with the money they were able to make restitution to their victims and still keep some for their own living expenses. I was very pleased to hear that.

In one of the prisons in southern Taiwan, because the weather was so hot, I came up with an idea of utilizing solar power, and asked them to collect related information quickly. We procured bids for installations, estimated our minimum annual power output, and how much of it we could sell to Taiwan Power Company and how much profit we could keep. Our project actually would pay for itself with the power generated; however, despite our wishful thinking, according to the accounting rule, we would have to turn over all our revenues to the state's coffers.

A manager now complained, "If we are not going to keep any money, what's the point of working so hard on this?" Even so, I believed we needed to persevere.

"There are two reasons why we needed to do this. First, the money would be going to the Treasury Department, which is our country. Secondly, we will be able to cool the temperature for the inmates. When the sun hits the flat roofs of the buildings it can get really hot. In the evenings, when inmates are in their rooms, the heat is still unbearable. Let's put ourselves in their shoes, and we shall know how they feel. We still must do it."

Shortly after I was transferred to another facility, I heard they had begun the project and were already generating power up to 10,000 kWh. They invited me to attend their celebration ceremony, but I declined, saying, "No need! No need! You guys are handling this well!" The fruits of our labor will remain in people's hearts, and I feel good for having done something right.

This time, I was in charge of yet another prison. There, seeing the male dormitories and the rooms for visiting families, I asked the head supervisor, "If your children were to live in such squalor, what would you say?" The place was horrible. The windows were bare without curtains, plastered only with newspapers. The beds were misshaped, too. The staff quarters were no better. New employees, seeing this, would choose to rent a place somewhere else instead of living on the premise. Thus, I set out to improve the environment, because only clean and ventilated space will clear away the polluted air within us; and only bright windows will let in light and retain employees. My wife and I would walk around the buildings every day to see what else we could improve.

Not only do we want to improve the environment, we also strive to lift up the inmates' spirits. Tzu Chi's culinary team came to teach the inmates how to cook vegetarian meals, thereby fostering respect for life and love of the earth. They also discovered that none of the female inmates knew how to cook. Life education, such as study groups, calligraphy classes, and rehabilitation seminars were offered with the hope of motivating and encouraging the prisoners to reform their ways.

I did not come from a wealthy family, and as a result have become quite frugal. In prison, if I can save a penny, I will. I watch the budget very closely. Ballpoint pens are one example. I buy them in bulk, two or three hundred dozen once or twice a month, but I am told that the staff gets a new pen each month. I do not think that is right. A pen should last two to three months even if used every day.

The people working on the night shift only use it to sign in. How can they need a new pen every month? That is not right. We should watch even the small change.

It does not matter where I am being transferred to, I will take it with gratitude, give it all my effort to let the light shine, smile at the forgotten people, and help them hear the voice of their inner good.

The fact is, there is no smooth sailing in life. As a young man, I was always looking for fame and fortune. "It is not fair", I would complain. Despite all the hard work I had put in, I never seemed to get a promotion. That bothered me greatly. To be sure, I never asked my superior for a transfer or a new position. Even so, shouldn't he have seen how hard I had worked? Not only was I not promoted, I was transferred to a less important unit. I could not sleep for a month or two during that time. On the day of the transfer, I did not sleep. I sat up and contemplated. If I did not make any mistakes, how can things be so unreasonable? Right then, looking out the window, I saw the moon unselfishly shining on the earth. I reminded myself, "One should be fearful of not contributing to the common good." It is through the trials of heaven a real man is made. I believe my superiors must have their reasons. Why make it hard for them? Dharma Master Cheng Yen says, "Life will not always throw a good pitch, but an experienced batter is always ready to take a swing." Thinking that, I had a smile from the bottom of my heart.

"Thank you, Chief, for making it more convenient for me, allowing me to stay close to my home." The next morning when I went to see my superior, I smiled understandingly and showed gratitude. He was very surprised and nodded approvingly. I believe I did what was right. I should not care how high my position is. When one has gratitude, one's heart will be filled with lightness. I am still thankful that I could change my perspective.

A lot of things teach me patience. Sometimes when the chief talked nonsense to me, I would grin and bear it, never rebuking him. My granddaughter would tell me what a good temper I had. I told her that whenever she hears anything she does not like, she can just pretend she did not hear it. When she quarreled with her brother, I told her the same thing; just pretend he is reciting a sutra. Don't listen to him. Don't mind him. Go and take a nap. There will be new things to do tomorrow. Let it go. A neighbor once told me, "I really envy you. You can do so many things in your position. I would give five years of my life just to be in your shoes." Honestly, I have always been grateful for my good fortune. I am very grateful that over these years I have been able to shed the light of hope in the many places I have gone. Many things may require our active engagement in order to happen. We can retire anytime, but what's important is that even at an old age, we are still able to think of how we may be of service to others, and believing in that will bring strength and courage into our life.

Our legacy is not what we have gained in this lifetime but what we have given away.

Please keep your sense of humor when reading the following. Smile. Everyone messes up sometimes.

Throwing a tantrum is an unprofitable proposition, and it is a good business to turn insults into merits. For some people, though, they are always getting angry as a matter of habit. Bluntly speaking, they have never made the transition into adulthood, and this leaves them in limbo where temporary insanity reins indefinitely.

Epilogue

Transform One's Heart Energy into Positive

As the flame of our life begins to fade, if someone were to revitalize it with a breath of fresh air, we would be most profoundly grateful. It could be a new outlook on life or an epiphany that infuses us with joy and gratitude, but how long that inspiration remains still depends on how much effort we put in.

I once heard a Buddhist teacher say to a mother whose son was born mentally challenged, "I'd rather believe your son is a bodhisattva who is taking on the suffering of all the sentient beings." With that new perspective, the mother felt great relief.

How is it that someone gets to be born into a world of tears and misery? Sometimes, the victim becomes the aggressor, and the cycle of violence continues because they have come to know violence as the only option. To protect themselves, they would resort to violence as they do not know any other way. By examining closely at our emotions, we can sometimes see clues to the reasons behind our actions. Crimes mostly begin with a distorted view of life.

In one of my talks, I used the funny stories of mental patients in an attempt to lighten up the audience. Unexpectedly, someone came to me afterward and said, "Don't you know how much these patients' families suffer? The daily hell they go through?" Right away, I felt so ashamed for not having the empathy for their families. I quickly put my palms together and thanked him for his timely reminder. We rarely give any thoughts on how the patients' families think. The joke takes only three minutes to tell, but their families must endure the ceaseless drama and emotional anguish on a daily basis.

This made me think of the inmates whose families must suffer untold amount of emotional distress. As we learn their stories, we might think, "If I were the inmate, what would happen to the people around me?" While documenting what the prison counselors' interactions with the inmates, I have also learned to step back and be more observant and sensitive about people's feelings. It is as if I were looking at myself from another person's perspective and seeing if I have gained more kindness and compassion.

The prison counselors and supervisors all wish for a more harmonious society. To that end, they have spent a great deal of effort promoting inmates' mental health and emotional well-being, helping them reconcile with their families and people, and together coming up with ways to ameliorate the emotional traumas they caused their victims' and their own families, and at the same time striving to be of benefit to people. It is as if the lamps behind the high walls are illuminating both the ground and their hearts, showing them the path.

The criminal law in the old days was more of a system of isolation and punishment. However, since the mid-1970s, law enforcement officers and victim groups began to notice the problem of the victims' having a diminished role under the old system as being useful only as witnesses. To help the victims and their families have a voice under the system, and to help the offenders see the harm they have caused the victims, Canada, New Zealand have begun adopting customs of the indigenous groups in restorative justice.

Restorative justice, according to Wikipedia, is based on the idea of "peace-making." It is argued that the handling of criminal cases should not be based solely on legal opinions but also on the basis of "social conflicts," "interpersonal relationship conflicts" basis to face the crime issue. Emphasizing the restoration of "social relations" means that the rights and dignity of the parties concerned should be met and the damaged relations between individuals, groups and communities should also be properly restored. In other words, social reintegration involves not only offenders, but also criminal policy that both the victims and the community need to be re-established so that all parties can return to normal life at the earliest through a program that is fair to both sides under the protection of the state system. Restoration justice must avoid coercing or deceiving the victims to let the offenders off the hook easily, and prevent the offenders from pretending to be reformed; in particular, unforgivable crimes such as sexual assault, manslaughter or abuse can traumatize the victims and their family and cause severe mental illnesses which are hard to heal and control, and the victims suffer for life. Restitution justice should be used with caution, especially when crimes committed to the victims and their family are serious; otherwise, restitution justice will become a mockery to the victims, passing out light sentences to serious crimes, and encouraging more offenses, tantamount to suppressing crime reports.

Dharma Master Cheng Yen says, "Illuminating the way is a symbol of light." It is hoped that we not only raise the lanterns during the Lantern Festival, but always keep the flames of wisdom alive. We shall bring light not only to our hearts, but to pass on the lanterns and illuminate the way for everyone else.

國家圖書館出版品預行編目 (CIP) 資料

心光有愛：映照生命的幽谷 / 林幸惠撰文 .-- 初版
臺北市：經典雜誌，慈濟傳播人文志業基金會，2018.04
面；　公分

　　ISBN 978-986-6292-96-5(平裝)

1. 更生保護 2. 心靈 3. 勵志
548.78　　　　　　　　　107002667

心光有愛：映照生命的幽谷

作　　　者／林幸惠

英文翻譯／張恭逢（**Richard Chang**）

英文協力／盧明哲、湯耀洋

中文修訂／林錫嘉、賴文玲、蔣佳珍、李芝、吳淇羚

聽打志工／北區人文真善美

發 行 人／王端正

總 編 輯／王志宏

叢書主編／蔡文村

叢書編輯／何祺婷

美術指導／邱宇陞

美術編輯／黃靜薇

出 版 者／經典雜誌

　　　　　財團法人慈濟傳播人文志業基金會

地　　址／台北市北投區立德路二號

電　　話／（**02**）**2898-9991**

劃撥帳號／**19924552**

戶　　名／經典雜誌

製版印刷／禹利電子分色有限公司

經 銷 商／聯合發行股份有限公司

地　　址／新北市新店區寶橋路 **235** 巷 **6** 弄 **6** 號 **2** 樓

電　　話／（**02**）**2917-8022**

出版日期／**2018** 年 **3** 月初版

　　　　　2020 年 **12** 月三版二刷

定　　價／新台幣 **320** 元

ISBN 978-986-6292-96-5（平裝）

Printed in Taiwan